Praise for **THE LIFE WE'RE LOOKING FOR**

"*The Life We're Looking For* is, and this is saying something, Andy Crouch's best book: a deeply moving meditation on the human need to find true personhood, which means, among other things, to know as we are known."

—ALAN JACOBS, author of
How to Think and *Breaking Bread with the Dead*

"Technology is, and always has been, both an opportunity and a threat to human flourishing. This short and profound book finds the middle way—the right way forward—through personhood, community, and love."

—TYLER VANDERWEELE, director of the
Human Flourishing Program at Harvard University

"In this truly brilliant book, Crouch uncovers why more and more people feel themselves to be living in an impersonal, unsatisfying, and lonely world. Filled with insightful analysis and wise counsel, *The Life We're Looking For* takes us into the heart of a more meaningful, shared, and joyous life that is inspired by the love of God. Reading it, you will discover what it takes to be human."

—NORMAN WIRZBA, Duke Divinity School
professor, author of *This Sacred Life*

"As I read this breathtaking book, I was surprised to find myself tearing up often. Surprised, that is, because it is not a book about tragedy or loss. But as I read, I realized that my tears flowed because Crouch, perhaps more than any other writer of our day, perceives and names the deepest and most vulnerable longings of the human heart. *The Life We're Looking For* describes the confusion, contradictions, frustrations, and dilemmas of our cultural moment in clear and resonant ways, and, more importantly, it offers hope that we might find a profoundly beautiful way of living amidst them. Crouch's depth of understanding, practical brilliance, and compelling vision of human wholeness and flourishing is evident on every page."

—TISH HARRISON WARREN, Anglican priest, author of *Liturgy of the Ordinary* and *Prayer in the Night*

"With warmth and erudition, *The Life We're Looking For* engages readers in a personal meditation on the hidden costs of our technological dreams. What are we not seeing, hearing, tasting, experiencing because we have partnered with devices? What would it take to insist that personal technologies become personal instruments of wonder? Crouch asks us to summon the intelligence, resolve, and faith to regain lost ground."

—SHERRY TURKLE, MIT professor, bestselling author of *Reclaiming Conversation* and *The Empathy Diaries*

"None of us can build a joyful and well-lived life alone. We are in this together, and becoming fully human persons is a collective project. Crouch offers real help for that problem by giving us a potent reframe to restore our personhood—individually and collectively. His artfully deep empathy dive on the true nature of persons and technology's impact upon us can empower us to better design a pathway to becoming our true selves and nurturing others in that worthy project."

—DAVE EVANS, cofounder of the Stanford Life Design Lab, bestselling coauthor of *Designing Your Life*

"Crouch's trustworthy voice diagnoses our culture and gives a vision for us to redeem it. He is a leader of leaders, and I'm grateful he stays out in front of the pack issuing wisdom."

—JENNIE ALLEN, bestselling author of *Get Out of Your Head*, Founder of IF:Gathering

"Technology that promised to bring us together is driving us apart. Crouch doesn't offer cheap slogans or easy fixes. Instead, he works to understand the roots of our alienation and despair. He gets the big picture of our digital age and helps families navigate the day-to-day. A thought-provoking look at the subtle, daily tradeoffs all of us make—between comfort and fulfillment, between shallow connection and deep relationship—and how we can push back against the forces pulling us apart."

—BEN SASSE, U.S. senator, bestselling author of *Them*

THE LIFE WE'RE LOOKING FOR

THE LIFE
WE'RE
LOOKING
FOR

RECLAIMING RELATIONSHIP
IN A TECHNOLOGICAL WORLD

———————————————————•

ANDY
CROUCH

CONVERGENT | NEW YORK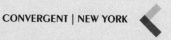

Published in the United States by Convergent Books, an imprint of Random House, a division of Penguin Random House LLC, New York.

CONVERGENT BOOKS is a registered trademark and its C colophon is a trademark of Penguin Random House LLC.

Library of Congress Cataloging-in-Publication Data
Names: Crouch, Andy, author.
Title: The life we're looking for / Andy Crouch.
Other titles: Life we are looking for
First Edition. | New York: Convergent Books, an imprint of Random House, [2022] |
Identifiers: LCCN 2021060334 (print) |
LCCN 2021060335 (ebook) | ISBN 9780593237342 (hardcover) |
ISBN 9780593237359 (ebook)
Subjects: LCSH: Communities—Religious aspects. |
Technology—Social aspects. | Alienation (Social psychology) |
Interpersonal relations.
Classification: LCC HM756 .C75 2022 (print) |
LCC HM756 (ebook) | DDC 302—dc23/eng/20220207
LC record available at https://lccn.loc.gov/2021060334
LC ebook record available at https://lccn.loc.gov/2021060335

Printed in the United States of America on acid-free paper

crownpublishing.com

1 2 3 4 5 6 7 8 9

First Edition

Book design by Elizabeth A. D. Eno

CONTENTS

THE LIFE WE'RE LOOKING FOR

WHAT WE THOUGHT
WE WANTED

The Loneliness of a Personalized World

Recognition is the first human quest.

After an ordinary delivery, after the first few startled cries, newborn infants typically spend an hour or so in the stage doctors call "quiet alert." Though they can only focus their vision roughly eight to twelve inches away, their eyes are wide open. They are searching, with an instinct far deeper than intention. They are looking for a face, and when they find one—especially a face that gazes back at them—they fix their eyes on it, having found what they were most urgently looking for.

Recognition is the primary task of infancy. Feeding, crying, and even sleeping are just the support system for this most essential work of figuring out who we are, and where we are, by making contact with other people, seeing them seeing us, gradually beginning to build our sense of self through their eyes.

As we nursed, our eyes found another pair of eyes and held on to them. When we were handed over to a father or a grandmother or an aunt or a cousin, we found their faces as well, gradually distinguishing them from one another. We looked at them with the steady, uninterrupted gaze of a baby, and because we were a baby—so very helpless and so very unable to cause harm, with those magnificently large eyes and that impossibly soft skin—they looked back at us with that same endless attention, unhindered and unafraid.

I know this happened for you, as it happened for me, because if it had not, you would almost certainly not be reading these words. The developmental psychologist Edward Tronick demonstrated this in a widely replicated experiment called "still face," in which infants and toddlers sit across from their caregivers, who have been told to avoid all facial expressions and responses to their children. The videos of these experiments, which last only a few minutes, are wrenching to watch, as the adults feign indifference to the children's presence while the children exhibit greater and greater degrees of dysregulation, writhing in frustration and ultimately collapsing in distress. That is the result of just a few moments of deprivation. When children are deprived of this kind of recognition and mutual attention for months or years, they may possibly survive—but they do not thrive.

Some children, of course, arrive in the world mysteriously and tragically lacking the neurological preparation for recognition. For six years, James, the son of my friends Peter and Ellie, lived a life sustained by love—but James could not name it, see it, or return it. He did not seem to notice or need a parent's gaze.

Then, on his seventh birthday, with no forewarning, James looked straight at his mother and said with slow, stammering effort, "Mom-my," then once again, "Mommy," then over and over with greater confidence and delight, "Mommy, Mommy, Mommy."

Ellie generally avoided using her smartphone in James's presence, but this one day she happened to have it in her hand and, prompted by some mother's instinct, had started a recording. When Peter played it for me, we both wept.

Not all such early moments of recognition are so memorable, but some part of us, I believe, remembers them all. Our own firstborn woke up in the middle of the night for the first few months, wanting to nurse. After he was fed, I would walk with him back and forth in the hallway of our apartment, lit by the glow of the streetlights outside. Though part of me desperately wanted him to be asleep, he was instead quiet and alert, looking intently at me.

He is a man now. It has been many years since he held my gaze that way. Nor does he need to—he is making his own way into the world. Perhaps one day he will look at a child the way I looked at him. But without those early days of regarding each other, recognizing each other, he would not have become who he is today. Because it was in those early days of life that he learned from my face and others' faces that he was a person. At the deepest layer of his sense of self, entirely lost to his conscious memory but buried as deep as the foundation stone of a building, are those nights with me in the hallway, quiet and alert, held and beloved.

FACIAL RECOGNITION

I pick up my phone and it stirs to life, looking for my face. Cameras focus silently, chips powered by machine learning swiftly compare images and patterns. The manufacturer has designed a little whirling animation on the screen to let me know that the process is under way. Moments later, a check mark appears in a circle and I'm in. I've been recognized.

This is, for now, one of our everyday moments of technological wonder, though our grandchildren will no more wonder or be astonished by it than we are by the light coming on when we flip the switch. It is, computationally speaking, a remarkable achievement. The capacity to recognize a face takes up a substantial part of the human brain, evolved over millions of years. In a few decades, we have managed to train our computers to approximate this capacity to the point that our machines can, in a sense, recognize us.

This technological progress unlocks our phones, and it unlocks new paradigms for computing as well, as devices become increasingly capable of recognizing our voices, our intentions, and even our emotions. There is every reason to believe that this progress will accelerate for the foreseeable future, giving us ever more accurate simulations of personalized interaction with our environment. These simulations will undoubtedly be useful, but maybe more importantly they will be satisfying—they will respond, in a way that early computers almost totally failed to do, to our very human need to be recognized and known.

Already our devices increasingly compete with real persons for our attention. A friend of mine went to visit his one-year-old niece. She had recently learned the word *no*—and was using it most stridently when people in the room started to look at their phones rather than remaining engaged with one another. Even the slightest glance at a screen would prompt urgent cries of "No! No! No!" from his niece—a real-world replay of Tronick's "still face" experiments.

"And yet," he told me, "I still found myself sneaking glances at my phone." The personalized world of the screen somehow held a power over his attention that the child before him did not—even as she cried, "No! No! No!"

PERSONALIZATION WITHOUT PERSONS

Not long ago, a handwritten envelope, addressed to "The Crouch Family," arrived in the mail. The letterforms had the exuberant artistry of a high schooler who likes to journal and send cards to her friends. The postmark was from a neighboring town. Who, I wondered, had taken the time to write us such a charming note?

Inside, written in the same friendly script on ruled yellow paper, was a note from "Sarah G.," who turned out to be a regional representative for a window company. She had thoughtfully included her business card, with another hand-scrawled note in blue ink on the reverse, inviting me to call for a no-obligation quote.

It was only after much careful and suspicious inspection that I concluded, as you've already guessed, that every one of my neighbors had probably also received a handwritten letter from Sarah G. There was no imprint on the page from the pressure of a pen—her casual printing was a convincing forgery produced by a high-definition inkjet printer, employing advanced techniques to imitate a real person's handwriting. Sarah G. had sent me a personalized letter—but not a personal one.

There is a consequential difference between *personalized* and *personal*. Personalized letters are sent by machines, not persons. Or they are sent by people so busy that they are functioning like machines—like the quick notes many American families inscribe on their holiday cards to far-flung friends.

Sarah G.'s letter, though perhaps a bit creepy, may seem essentially benign. Like all the best advertising, it aimed to alert me to a product I might very well need. Her perfectly personalized messages were sent to certain homeowners, in a certain zip code, with a certain economic and social profile—the kind of people who not only desire new windows but can afford them.

Those of us who fit the profile are on the receiving end of a blizzard of personalization—promotional emails that reference prior purchases, eerily specific online ads for products we've been considering, app notifications timed to match the times of day we're most likely to make a purchase. Is that such a bad thing? The more personalized our world becomes, it might seem, the more suited it is for our flourishing. And it is not just advertisers who tailor their offerings to our interests, needs, and identity. We do the same with our "curated" news feeds and carefully personalized home screens. All this personalization is exactly what makes our technology so alluring—enough to draw our attention away from even the most insistent one-year-old.

A personal encounter with a one-year-old, after all, may well involve me in conversations or activities that I will quickly find repetitive or boring. The technologies at the frontier of personalization, on the other hand, are exquisitely attuned to my attention span. My feeds from Twitter and Instagram, along with the well-timed ads from merchants whose sites I recently browsed, are finely calibrated to my interests, my need for novelty and stimulation, even my particular insecurities and fantasies. While Sarah G.'s epistle was poorly informed (our windows are actually a decade or more from needing replacement), the more advanced forms of personalization sometimes seem to know me better than I know myself,

recommending entertainment, news, and music that perfectly tickle my own particular taste buds.

These personalized encounters can be thrilling in their
transactional simplicity. Because there is no actual person
on the other side of them, the only person who has to
be taken into account is me—glorious me! My interests,
my priorities, my preferences, my agenda—all are being
processed and presented to me in a cascade of reflections
far more captivating than Narcissus's pool. And all this
is happening without the complication, frustration, per-
plexity, unpredictability, and vulnerability of encountering another person with their own needs, expectations,
anxieties, and desires.

It is, in fact, a one-year-old's dream—because if we
are truthful, as heart-wrenching as it is, the "No! No!
No!" of my friend's niece is not just a desire for connection. It is also a desire to be in charge, to have what she
wants when she wants it, to master others' affection and
attention. It is dawning on her that other faces do not
always seek out her own, that others are not always there
to satisfy her needs. She is discovering that a personal
world—a world of persons—can be a difficult and disap-
pointing place.

And unless her parents and caregivers make choices
that are increasingly radical in our world of personalized
devices, very soon, probably at one of these moments of
distress, someone will offer her a screen. It will light up
at her touch; it will always be within reach; it will offer
age-appropriate delights and diversions. Once again, she

will be at the center of everything—every one-year-old's dream come true. The room will be quiet, her parents will be disburdened, a kind of peace will be restored.

But all this will come at the expense of what she was looking for the day she was born, what we were all looking for—because before we knew to look for a mirror, we were looking for another person's face.

A LONELY PLANET

If there is one word that sums up the crisis of personhood in our time, for the powerful and powerless alike, it is *loneliness.* Like Ernest Hemingway's character who went broke "gradually and then suddenly," modern people and societies have suddenly become acutely aware that we are relationally bankrupt.

Physicians see it: Vivek Murthy, surgeon general of the United States under Presidents Barack Obama and Joe Biden, wrote in the *Harvard Business Review* in 2017, "During my years caring for patients, the most common pathology I saw was not heart disease or diabetes; it was loneliness."

Politicians see it: Ben Sasse, the Harvard-trained historian who became a U.S. senator for Nebraska, argued in his 2018 book, *Them: Why We Hate Each Other—and How to Heal,* that the actual root of the conflicted, polarized politics of the United States is loneliness. Prime Minister Theresa May of the United Kingdom appointed a cabinet minister for loneliness in 2018—a notable and noble gesture, though it is surely a position the most ambitious politicians will do their best to avoid.

Businesses see it, because there is big money in offsetting loneliness: "Objective social isolation" costs the U.S. Medicare system $6.7 billion annually, according to one study.

And the media certainly see it. Knowing that I was writing a book on technology and relationships, friends and family have deluged me with articles on loneliness, every one of which seems to include the dubiously calculated, certainly unprovable, but eye-catchingly memorable claim that loneliness is as bad for your health as smoking fifteen cigarettes a day.

Along with this claim, someone is sure to observe that "we have never been so connected—and never so lonely." And indeed, those of us who eagerly joined Facebook and other platforms during the social media explosion of the 2000s could hardly have imagined that we were actually going to feel more alienated, not less, all these years later. Is it coincidence, or just a kind of grand irony, that loneliness has spiked just as our media became "social," our technology became "personal," and our machines learned to recognized our faces?

In fact, this is no coincidence. Our relational bankruptcy has been unfolding through the five-hundred-year story of technology, from its earliest stirrings in Europe in the fifteenth and sixteenth centuries to Silicon Valley in the twenty-first. There is a consistent shadow side of the bright promises and genuine achievements of the technological world: It has been based all along on a false understanding of what human beings really are and what we most need. We thought we were looking for impersonal power, the kind that doesn't need persons to be effective. And now we have it, with everything we want delivered straight to our doorstep by processes and systems we scarcely understand employing persons we never see—or who, in cases like Sarah G., may actually not exist.

If you picked up this book, chances are you feel it too: that this dream that began so pleasantly is, like so many dreams, beginning to spin out of control. There must be a different and better life to seek, a different and better way to be persons, a different and better way to deploy all the knowledge, wealth, and power that we have spent on our shallow, mirrored selves.

And in fact, alongside the gradual and sudden development of our personalized impersonal world, another story has been playing itself out, a story not of bankruptcy but of redemption, in which, rather than persons dwindling into anonymity, the anonymous and neglected have found recognition and been recalled to life. This book is about how we can rejoin that story—about how, in an impersonal world, it is still possible to become persons again.

RECLAIMING PERSONHOOD

Sometime in the early 50s—not our 1950s but the literal 50s of the common era, early in the reign of the notorious Roman emperor Nero—roughly half a dozen persons gathered around a table in the Greek city of Corinth. Two millennia later, we know much less about each of them than we would like, but they themselves knew one other intimately. So intimately, in fact, that they called one another by family names, "sister" and "brother," even though any passerby who heard them using that language would have been mystified, if not horrified.

For they were not in any way related to one another—in fact, in any ordinary time they should never have met at all.

We will learn a little more about them in the course of this book, but we should start with this: They were gathered in the house of a man named Gaius. While his proper name tells us little about him—there were Gaiuses everywhere in the Roman world—it is enough, to gauge his rank and station, to know that he was a man with a house, and not a small one. He was a *paterfamilias,* the head of a Roman household, a citizen of a strategically located colonial city.

When modern Americans meet someone for the first time, we quickly ask, "So what do you do?" But well-born Romans did not ask that question because in Roman society the question was not *what* but *who*—not your occupation but your relations. What would have mattered most about Gaius to his neighbors was that he was a client to men more powerful than himself and a patron to others less powerful, embedded in a web of obligations and favors that granted him dignity and status.

There is one other significant thing about Gaius that we need to grasp in order to understand the strange gathering of "brothers" and "sisters" who were under his roof—and the relevance of their gathering so long ago for us and our time.

He was a person.

Well, that's obvious, you may well say. Everyone is a person, right?

Not exactly. Not in Gaius's world. And if we're being honest, not in many parts of the world today.

We actually get the word *person* from Gaius's time. The Latin word *persona* initially referred to the masks used in ancient theater. It then came to mean the role an actor played (many plays today still indicate their cast with the phrase *dramatis personae,* the characters of the drama). But by Gaius's time the word had a legal meaning. It referred to someone with standing before the law, someone whom the law protected and courts could judge.

Many people in Gaius's world were, in fact, not persons in this sense. Slaves, above all, though they were undeniably human, were treated under the law not as persons but as property (*res* in Latin, the simple word for "thing" or, as we might say today, "stuff"). Perhaps 20 percent of the population of the Roman Empire were enslaved—not generally on account of their race, as in the slavery that stains American history, but because of defeat in battle or debt they had not been able to repay.

Noncitizens, also, lacked the full status of persons—for example, if they were accused of a crime, they could be whipped and tortured with impunity to obtain evidence. Women and children had legal personhood only in relation to their *paterfamilias,* the head of the household to which they belonged by birth or by marriage.

These were not just legal formalities. To be a *persona* was to count for something in the public world. Every human being may *be* a person, then and now. But everywhere Gaius went, he was *recognized* as a person. And when it comes to flourishing as a person, recognition makes all the difference.

Gaius's social world was what sociologists call "stratified"—marked by clear and seemingly unbridgeable divides. As often in history, this stratification was actually increased and solidified by the Roman Empire's material prosperity, which had seen a vast expansion of wealth powered by advances in agriculture, engineering, finance, and more. But it was a time, like ours, where the benefits of that prosperity were very unevenly distributed and where personhood was hard to find—even, in a way, for *paterfamiliae* like Gaius. It was hard work to maintain one's connections, status, and recognition in an ever more complex and urbanizing empire. The Roman Empire was a lonely place for almost everyone, powerless or powerful.

Yet in Gaius's house, a social movement was beginning that would, over a few centuries, turn the notion of personhood in the Roman world upside down. Even as the technological and economic power of the Roman Empire continued to grow, a most unlikely set of *dramatis personae* was taking the stage. They had come to believe, against all evidence and social convention—and for a long time, in the face of relentless cultural and political repression—that they were in fact fully persons and that they had discovered the way to a flourishing life together.

Around tables where men like Gaius would normally recline, drink, and dine, waited upon by slaves and titillated by entertainers, fledgling groups connected to this movement in cities around the Mediterranean—groups of men and women, Jews and Greeks, slaves and free— enjoyed a very different kind of meal. In halls that were accustomed to feasts that signaled the status and significance of the host, this community would pass a single loaf of bread from hand to hand, in remembrance of someone not present. In place of reverent toasts to the emperor, they would sing songs both ancient and new that spoke of a different king and kingdom.

And on the occasion we will consider most closely in this book, in a room where lengthy letters would normally be dictated and dispatched to contacts in distant cities to advance the interests of the sender, Gaius and his friends would witness the writing of a new kind of epistle—one that challenged almost all the assumptions of the Roman world, and the Jewish world as well, about the ideal human community, one in which every single member mattered as much as each part of our own bodies matters to us.

We desperately need a movement like this today.

This movement will start by acknowledging all the ways of being human we have lost as we have become embedded in a world of money, machines, and devices. It will require reconsidering the roots of the modern technological mindset, which turns out to be something built on harmful delusions, quite different from science itself. It will require giving a far more serious reckoning than we have generally allowed to the ancient, primal, and spiritual forces that still animate our technological dreams. That is the subject of the first half of this book, followed by a short "intermission" that looks in more detail at Gaius, his guests, and the social movement that was beginning among them.

And then, in the second half, we'll begin to imagine what I will call "redemptive moves"—the ways we can begin, right now, to live more fully human lives. We do not have to accept our technology's default settings— they can be adapted, and eventually redesigned, to serve a new and better set of purposes. We do not have to live in ever-increasing isolation. Our homes, like Gaius's, can become creative centers far more consequential than the refuges of consumption and leisure we have let them become. And from these new households, we can begin to extend the recognition of personhood to those most in danger of being overlooked.

The great news is that there are already examples of these redemptive moves—some seedlings, some saplings, some beginning to bear widespread fruit—and we all have a part to play in helping them grow.

This is not a mass movement—in fact, it never will be, because mass movements are by definition impersonal. All real change starts with the number of people who can sit around a table in a single household. But this movement can grow in ways we cannot fully imagine today— and we know that is true because the handful of persons who sat around Gaius's table are still shaping our world.

And while there is much to critique and criticize in our lonely civilization, this is a movement built on inextinguishable hope.

The quest for personal recognition, the hope that there is a face that is looking for us, begins again with every newborn child. We sometimes hear children born into our technological world called "digital natives." But there is really no such thing.

Every day, in the most apparently desperate and forsaken parts of our world, as well as the most affluent, distracted, and anxious parts, babies are being born, their eyes wide open, looking for a face. They hope, without yet knowing what hope is, that they are being born into a world where someone is looking for them—a world where they will be recognized, known, and loved, a world where they will have a glorious part to play, one of the *dramatis personae*.

And because all of us are born with that hope, the

hope of recovering personhood in our time is far from lost. There is no way back—for us, any more than for a baby delivered from the womb. But there is a way forward.

All this way requires is the willingness and courage, like that of the babies we once were, to search again for a face.

HEART, SOUL, MIND, STRENGTH

WHAT WE'VE FORGOTTEN
ABOUT BEING A PERSON

Before it was renamed after a legendary World War II pilot, Chicago's O'Hare International Airport was called Orchard Field, a charming name whose memory lingers in its airport code, ORD. For nearly ten years, I passed through that airport almost weekly. As I started those journeys, I would tell myself I was flying into Orchard Field, just to raise my spirits.

At the baggage claim and the arrivals curb, I would witness the full amplitude of human life: joyful reunions and tearful departures of spouses, grandparents, parents, and children (along with a fair amount of impatient screen-checking as business travelers waited for ride share vehicles). The external "landside" of an airport features relationship, motion, and purpose. But inside, beyond the security check, I would enter the travel dead zone, where everyone wanted to be somewhere else. In that limbo, I found my own appetite for reality, and life itself, shrinking. Much of the time, I joined my fellow travelers in retreating into the restless solitude of a glowing screen.

But one winter evening at O'Hare, I had one of the more memorable and moving spiritual experiences of my life.

On that night, I was at the far end of United Airlines' Terminal 1, with almost two hours to kill. Fearsome security lines made it impractical to go outside, but coming off several full days of meetings in conference rooms, it occurred to me that I hadn't had a proper walk, or any other real exercise, in days. Because the three domestic terminals at O'Hare are all connected behind security, I realized that I could get in several miles of walking if I traveled from one end to the other and back.

That would be my physical exercise for the night. But since an airport isn't the most sublime environment for a walk—one step up, perhaps, from covering the same distance on a treadmill—I needed something for my mind, and ideally my heart and soul as well.

I had recently been thinking about one of the most striking ways that the Hebrew Scriptures describe human beings: "made in the image of God," male and female, all part of one human family. Radical when it was first written down in Genesis, and still challenging today, it's an idea worth pondering.

It occurred to me that I could attempt a kind of ambulatory act of contemplation. As I walked, I decided, I would try to take note of each person I passed. I would pay as much attention to each of them as I could—as much, that is, without seeming like some kind of creepy airport stalker—and say to myself as I saw each one, *image bearer.*

I started out on my journey at a brisk pace, backpack cinched tight on my shoulders. I passed a weary-looking man in a suit. *Image bearer.* Right behind him was a woman in a sari. *Image bearer.* A mother pushed a stroller with a young baby; a young man, presumably the baby's father, walked next to her, half holding, half dragging a toddler by the hand. *Image bearer, image bearer, image bearer, image bearer.* A ramp worker walked by in a bulky coat and safety vest. *Image bearer.*

By the time I reached the corridor where Terminal 1 connects to Terminal 2, I had passed perhaps two hundred people, glancing at their faces just long enough to say to myself, *image bearer.* I had six more concourses to go. I walked down the length of Concourse E and back— *image bearer, image bearer, image bearer, image bearer.* Then F, then G, then H, then K. After about forty-five minutes of walking—*image bearer, image bearer, image bearer*—I was at the end of Concourse L (its most distant gates, fittingly, home of an airline notorious for cut-rate fares and cramped seats). A gate agent was checking in the last passengers on a plane to Fort Lauderdale. *Image bearer.*

Few of the people I passed looked genuinely happy or sad, but then, those emotions are generally reserved for the airport's outer courts. Instead, they looked, by turns, bored, anxious, patient, cautious, and faintly hopeful.

By the end of my walk, I was overwhelmed in a way I had not expected. I had passed people in every stage of life and health, of an uncountable number of national and ethnic backgrounds, some traveling together, most seemingly alone. The stories I would never learn behind each of those faces, the years of life that had shaped their posture and gait, the possibility and futility each one had known and would know—all set to the relentless soundtrack of those two words, *image bearer*—carried an emotional and spiritual weight that I can still feel, years later. From time to time I repeat this exercise on a city street, in a coffee shop, even driving on the highway where faces are just a blur behind a windshield. *Image bearer, image bearer, image bearer.* It never fails to move me and still me.

The late Leanne Payne, a teacher of the spiritual life, once said, "We either contemplate or we exploit." Exploitation asks, What can this person (or for that matter, this *thing*) do for me? Contemplation asks, *Who* or *what* am I beholding, without regard for their usefulness to me? My *image bearer* exercise was a small attempt to contemplate—to actually attend and behold and name the dignity of each person I passed. But the exercise also felt tragic, because while there is something elevating and hopeful about naming each person you pass in this way, there is also an inescapable sense of loss, of something unfulfilled, undiscovered, or perhaps abandoned long ago.

THE COST OF CONVENIENCE

The unexpected pathos of my evening at O'Hare is not, I hardly need to say, the ordinary reality of my life, or of almost anyone's life in our hurried, crowded world.

I stop by a convenience store on my way to work—the term itself a sign that its principal offering is not any inherent quality of the store's products or occupants but its usefulness to me. There are several people ahead of me in line to check out, and by the time I reach the cashier, I am conscious of my own impatience and the people who have joined the line behind me. The cashier swipes my items in front of a laser array, never attempting eye contact, as I wave my credit card over the reader. Were either of us called to identify each other an hour later, to pick each other out of a lineup of usual suspects, I am quite sure we would fail.

I hurry out of the store and get into my car, a few thousand pounds of metal and glass that give me extraordinary mobility and also extraordinary isolation from the people around me. The back-up camera shows a hazy view of a pedestrian crossing behind me as I wait—another person in my proximity I would never be able to recall even a moment later, as they register largely as a temporary waif on a screen. Once the way is clear, I pull out into traffic, where I am much more likely to recognize a car—the Ford Flex our family used to own, the Tesla I was reading about this week, the BMW I know I can't afford—than a face.

Occasionally there is an interruption in this seamless, faceless journey. Sometimes it is welcome—a child waving experimentally from the back seat at each vehicle that passes on the interstate, delighted by the waves she receives in return. Sometimes it is unsettling—waiting to turn left at a stoplight and seeing a frail human being standing in the median strip between six lanes of traffic, holding a sign that says HUNGRY. PLEASE HELP. I feel slightly exploited by this appeal to charity, resentful of his vulnerability and inclined to consider it a subtle kind of manipulation—but most of the time, as I avoid his gaze, I can't help feeling that he, more than anyone else in my daily commute, is actually looking at me, seeing me, attending to me, even if only in the hopes of receiving something from me. That feeling of actually being seen is somehow even more unsettling than my fellow drivers' anonymity or the cashier's indifference.

My life is full of convenience. It is full of transaction, at its best a mutually beneficial exchange of value, a kind of arm's-length benign use of one another for our own ends. But it is not full of contemplation. It is often efficient. But it is lonely.

My world is full of people, indeed more full than any human being before the last few crowded centuries could have possibly imagined. But it does not feel like a world of persons. In this small distinction between *people* and *persons* is condensed the story of what we have found and lost.

People is the most ordinary word (in American English at least) for a group of human beings. It is the word for a group too large to recognize individual faces, or a group whose members you do not know. When we are with "people," faces blur into a crowd. *Persons,* on the other hand, is an "each one" word—it somehow keeps in view the fact that each one in the room has a unique identity, story, and name. While we can also speak of *individuals,* isolating those identities like so many pebbles, *persons* holds them together. There is, however faintly, a hope attached to that somewhat unusual term *persons:* the acknowledgment and expectation that each of them could be known.

Of course, we cannot develop deep relationships with every one of the countless persons we interact with in the course of modern life. But our glancing encounters with one another can change when the uniquely contemplative word *person* is echoing even in the most impersonal environments. I call my insurance company to file a claim for a cracked windshield, expecting to exchange bits of routine information in the distant and wary tone of call-center conversations. But a glitch in the representative's system throws her momentarily off the script, I offer a word of sympathy for how often computers seem to slow down our work rather than speed it up, and suddenly we are laughing together, fellow persons in a sea of procedures and algorithms. By the end of the call, we are offering each other words of blessing for the day that is ahead. We will surely never meet face to face and most likely never talk again, but we have somehow ended this commercial transaction more awake and alive than when we began.

THE PARADOX OF PERSONHOOD

There are three truths we have to hold together about persons.

First, as the German philosopher Robert Spaemann put it, there is a difference between "something" and "someone." The difference is personhood. Philosophers might say it is *ontological*—rooted in our being—and *inalienable*—it cannot be taken away. As I walk through the airport, I do not have to discern which of the humans walking past me are persons. That tiny baby being carried by her parents, perhaps to meet her grandparents for the first time? She is a person. That young man, who perhaps flew overnight, who is sleeping, mouth agape, across two seats in the waiting area? He is a person. That elderly woman with a slightly anxious gaze, struggling to navigate the busy, noisy airport? She is a person. Nor is there any moral component to this judgment—everyone I see, no matter how nobly or poorly they are behaving, is a person.

You do not have to become a person. You do not have to prove you are a person. As long as you have been and as long as you will be, you are a person.

This would seem elementary and hardly worth mentioning, except for the brutal fact that there have been, and are, so many places and times where not just individuals, but whole communities of people, were not treated as persons at all. And even the most privileged among us have found our sense of personhood slipping. At certain places and times, we have sensed, even if we could not quite explain why, that we were being treated as *something* rather than *someone*. My conversation with the insurance representative began in a dull, distant monotone because both of us had been conditioned to expect yet another encounter that would reduce us to facts and functions.

So, while nothing can truly take away our personhood, only another person can fully give it to us. This is the second essential truth. It is when another person's face and voice recognize us, not for what we can offer them (exploitation) but for what we intrinsically are (contemplation), that we know who we are. We are meant to know that we are persons in and through the recognition of others. In the end, we are not individuals. Only when we know and are known by others can we become fully ourselves.

And this word, *fully,* leads us to the third truth. While personhood can be denied (though never truly taken away) and it can be gravely harmed, it also can be *de-*

veloped. There is tension, if not paradox, here: There is nothing you can do or become that makes you more or less of a person. But being a person means you are designed to become something greater than you are.

Persons are meant to grow. This is evident in childhood development, in the astonishing innate drive of children to establish mutual recognition, to learn to communicate, to join and participate in a family and community. But it is also evident in the things that draw and drive us as adults, above all our loves: the pursuits that the Greeks called *philia* (friendship and kinship) and *eros* (sex and romance), and to which the first Christians added *agapē* (self-giving and sacrifice). Insofar as all of these draw us into the lives of others, they are all schools of personhood, a lifelong invitation to a deeper and better life than we would know on our own.

To be a person is to be made for love. This is both the indelible fact of who we are and the great adventure of each of our lives.

And it is precisely this central task—becoming the relational beings we are meant to be—that is so desperately difficult in our technological, impersonal world. Walk through an airport, consider the persons you pass, and you will see.

HEART-SOUL-MIND-STRENGTH COMPLEXES DESIGNED FOR LOVE

To grasp what we are missing in our development as persons, we must revisit one of the single most durable ideas in human history—several millennia older than our technological society, and centuries older than the philosophers of Greece and Rome.

Some ideas are found only in books, but this one has been written down and literally nailed on the outside of millions of buildings, very likely including one within walking distance of the place where you live and work. But unless you are part of the community that has been the steward of this remarkable idea, you may well have no clue how to find it. It has been under our noses all along, waiting for us to take it seriously.

It begins with the words *Shema Israel*.

> Hear, O Israel: The LORD is our God, the LORD alone. You shall love the LORD your God with all your heart, and with all your soul, and with all your might. (Deut. 6:4–5)

This is the English translation of one of the most important texts in Jewish life, the text from the book of Deuteronomy whose first Hebrew word, *shema*, means "hear." A small scroll with these lines of Scripture, handwritten on special parchment by a trained scribe, is affixed to the doorpost of every observant Jewish home, rolled up inside a small ceremonial box called a mezuzah and nailed or glued (not velcroed, modern rabbis have had to clarify) at roughly shoulder height on the doorframe. The passage goes on to instruct, "Recite [these words] to your children and talk about them when you are at home and when you are away, when you lie down and when you rise. Bind them as a sign on your hand, fix them as an emblem on your forehead, and write them on the doorposts of your house and on your gates" (6:7–9).

The Shema gives us a vision of what it means to be a person—the fullness of life for which we were made. This vision emerged from a long discussion in Jewish life that started with a simple question: What is the greatest commandment? If you could pick a single mitzvah from the 613 the rabbis had identified in the Law, summing up what human beings were meant to be and become, what would it be?

On this question, unlike many others, there was wide consensus: It must be the commandment found at the heart of the Shema, the command to love God with all of one's heart, soul, and might. Jesus himself, when pressed by rabbinic leaders on this question, answered exactly the way that many other teachers of the Law would have done: "The first is, 'Hear, O Israel: the Lord our God, the Lord is one; you shall love the Lord your God with all your heart, and with all your soul, and with all your mind, and with all your strength.' The second is this, 'You shall love your neighbor as yourself'" (Mark 12:29–31).

In this answer, we see two notable additions to the

actual text of the Shema. The immediately noticeable one is adding the commandment, found in the book of Leviticus, to "love your neighbor as yourself," extending the love commanded toward God also in the direction of one's neighbor (which prompts the lawyer in Luke's gospel to ask Jesus his uneasy question, "And who is my neighbor?").

The other, more subtle addition is taking Deuteronomy's three categories of heart, soul, and strength, and adding *mind*—the unique human capacity for reflection and understanding—as one of the elements of full love of God and neighbor.

The Shema, as extended by Jesus, gives us a very compact summary of what being fully human involves. We see it out of the corner of our eye when we read the Shema, but let's put it right in the center, definition-style, so that we can pay close attention to what it may mean for our time:

> Every human person is a heart-soul-mind-strength complex designed for love.

A human person is not a mind without a heart. You are not a brain without a body. You are not a body without a soul, nor were you ever meant to be a soul without a body. You are all of these, together, and it is this complex of qualities that makes you a person. Each of us is a combination of several parts that add up to something more.

We are *heart*—driven and drawn by desire. Our choices

are shaped not just by thought but also emotion. We pursue things (and persons) that are beautiful, but we also can be moved by passion and compassion toward things (and persons) that are vulnerable. We feel and act on these feelings long before we think—as in the instinctual swerve of a driver avoiding a tiny creature darting across the road, or the instantaneous choice to jump into the surf to save a drowning child.

We are *soul*—we have a depth of self that is uniquely ours, recognizably different from any other, a reality interior to us and only partly available to others. Once in a while, if we are lucky, we may find someone who feels like our "soul mate"—someone who seems to instinctively understand the depths of who we are without our needing to put it into words. Yet even these persons will never fully know us, and indeed, the wiser we become, the less we feel that we fully know ourselves.

We are *mind*—capable, far more than any other creature, of reflecting on the world, remembering and interpreting our experience, and analyzing it. Even as small children we ask, "Why?" The desire for knowledge is matched only by the delight that comes when we find that the world does indeed make a kind of beautiful sense, whether in the rhythm and rhymes of a great poem or the mathematical elegance of the planets' orbits. We not only seek truth, but from time to time, we feel sure we have found it.

And we are *strength*—capable of applying great energy toward work as well as play. The Hebrew *me'od* is not limited to the physical—it could be translated "muchness," the fullness of the self—but it certainly includes our physical constitution. We are not as agile as a cat, fast as a gazelle, or strong as an ox, but we combine agility, speed, and strength in a way that few other creatures do. A person who trains the body diligently can acquire not only the gross-motor ability to complete a triathlon but also the fine-motor skills to sew or to play the violin. Our bodies have obvious limits. But they are a marvel, especially when animated by heart, soul, and mind. We are fearfully and wonderfully made.

Most of all, we are designed for love—primed before we were born to seek out others, wired neurologically to respond with empathy and recognition, coming most alive when we are in relationships of mutual dependence and trust. Love calls out the best in us—it awakens our hearts, it stirs up the depths of our souls, it focuses our minds, it arouses our bodies to action and passion. It also calls out what is most human in us. Of all the creatures on earth, we are by far the most dependent, the most relational, the most social, and the most capable of care. When we love, we are most fully and distinctively ourselves.

So, at least, is the testimony of the great wisdom traditions of the world, of which the Jewish religion is one of the most durable and influential.

And yet there is another truth we discover very early on in our lives: We are not at all what we were meant to be.

THE BABY'S FRUSTRATION

In recent years researchers have cataloged the extraordinary burst of mental activity that accompanies our first years of life. Typical babies will learn the syntax and the working vocabulary of an entire human language by age three—and if they are exposed to a second language, they will acquire it with no apparent additional effort. It's not too much to say that whatever your accomplishments since then, one of the most impressive achievements of your life was already complete by the time you started school.

And while babies have very little command over their bodies and little physical strength compared to full-grown human beings, that is not really what the Hebrew word *me'od* is about. It is about fullness of effort— "muchness"—and in this, babies absolutely excel. Everything they do, they do physically, fully, and most often exuberantly.

The command of the Shema is, in a way, simply a call to return to the "allness" that characterized the beginning of our lives. We once did this without having to be taught: the unselfconscious full gift of the self to others and to the task of growing and becoming in the world. Unless we had exceptional limitations, every one of us once danced. Every one of us sang and learned melody and music without the slightest hesitation. Every one of us drew and painted, with fingers or with pencil or with brush. And if circumstances did limit our ability to do these things in the way typical children would have done, in some ways our "allness" was even more amazing in our drive to overcome and compensate for our limitations. To the extent that we were loved, we were free.

But, of course, this is what happened to us: the recognition and love we had so instinctively and fearlessly sought was, sooner or later, nowhere to be found.

The psychiatrist Curt Thompson speaks movingly about this fundamental human drama. Even in the most loving homes—in fact, a home is not fully loving if this does *not* happen—the parent withdraws. They leave the room for a moment; they leave the house for a day. The face and presence that anchored the child's sense of self is gone.

If all is well, the parent returns, and the dance of persons—each responding to the other in full—is reestablished. But the drama has been set in motion. What do we do when the persons who matter most in our life depart? How, then, do we know who we are? And what will we do if they do not return?

Soon enough, even in relatively healthy homes, we learn that all is not well. We begin to experience episodes of others' anger, rejection, and shame. And we also discover that it is not just the other who can be absent or angry—we, too, desire to escape and to hide. We learn, amazingly early, how to rupture a relationship. And this is not confined to childish tantrums. Well into adulthood we find ourselves lashing out at those who anger us and withdrawing from those who frustrate us.

All this happens in the healthiest of families. But very often, absence and anger escalate into various forms of abuse and violence. And even if our own family of origin is relatively free of these disruptions to the love we were seeking, as we come of age, we discover that the world cannot always be trusted to recognize us as persons. After injuries small and great, we may begin to wonder whether the love we assumed was our birthright can be found at all.

We also discover, though we may never put words to this discovery, that the world we have inherited seems almost designed to cut us off from the heart-soul-mind-strength fullness we were wired for at birth. This strange alienation applies on both sides of the modern world's vast inequities—there is a deprivation of the slums, but there is also a deprivation of the suburbs. Both environments are cut off from much of the natural world our ancestors knew; both are filled, in different ways, with manufactured material; both buzz with busyness, distraction, and various kinds of self-medication. Both are crowded with human activity, and at the same time both are strangely lonely.

Lacking depth of connection with others and God, the reciprocal relations in which "deep calls to deep," we lose our sense of soul and self. Our minds drift and wander, seeking comfort and familiarity rather than challenge and creativity. Our strength atrophies—how many of us can say that we maintain a healthy pattern of exertion and fatigue, work and rest? Instead, we fall into vicious cycles of inactivity and lethargy.

And so one day we find ourselves in the dead zone of an airport, or perhaps in a whole world that feels like a dead zone—a place where we are never recognized, where no one knows our names, where no one names our souls. We feel our hearts, souls, minds, and strength dwindling—or perhaps they have dwindled so much we do not even notice.

The honest truth is that often, we just give in. We make choices that accelerate the patterns of emptiness and loneliness rather than reverse them. And thanks to a particularly tricky design feature of our heart-soul-mind-strength complex, it can initially seem that these small consolations and addictions offer us just enough of what we long for to get by. Human beings have made these kinds of choices ever since the pain of being persons was first felt. But today, we happen to have access to a way out of disappointment that offers more false comfort than our ancestors could ever have imagined.

Let's call it the superpower zone.

THE SUPERPOWER ZONE

How We Trade Personhood for Effortless Power

I live on a suburban street about a third of a mile long, lined with houses and sidewalks, frequented by joggers and children on bicycles, and interrupted midway by an intersection with a stop sign. It is a street perfectly suited to its posted speed limit, twenty-five miles per hour. And yet every day I see automobiles that reach thirty-five to forty miles per hour as they pass our house, driven not only by restless adolescents or people who are late to work but also by persons of all sorts and conditions.

Strictly speaking, the bursts of speed I witness offer no practical benefit. Exceeding the speed limit on an interstate highway can save you real time in reaching a distant destination; speeding on our little street won't save even the fastest driver more than a few seconds, end to end.

It's irrational—but nearly irresistible. I know because I sometimes find myself pulling out of our driveway and accelerating briskly up our little street to the stop sign I know is only one block away.

There is something about the accelerator pedal of a car that gives us a sense of control and exhilaration, autonomy and liberation. On the right kind of day, it is a compensation for the frustrations of being human. With just a slight inflection of our foot, we exercise heedless power. It costs us nothing, physically, but it rewards us with a jolt of energy that feels almost spiritual.

Almost all of human history was carried on at the speed of roughly three miles an hour—the speed of walking. The Japanese theologian Kosuke Koyama provocatively called three miles an hour "the speed of God" since it was the speed at which Jesus of Nazareth moved for almost his entire life. Before the invention of modern engines, any increase in speed above this natural threshold would have taken notable physical effort—the exertion of the sprinter or the endurance of the marathon runner, the counterpoised strength and balance of horse and rider, the sailor harnessing the wildness of the wind on the ocean.

But, of course, human beings dreamed of more—or really, more and less. More speed, less effort. More power, less risk. A bird soaring on currents of air glides seemingly without effort, and that is what we, too, imagined, whether in the cautionary tale of Icarus or the delicate and detailed designs of Leonardo da Vinci.

We dreamed of effortless speed. And now everyone who drives down our little street has it.

POWERS AND SUPERPOWERS

Effortless power is one of the most distinctive features of what we began, roughly 150 years ago, to call "modern" life. In countless domains, technology has equipped human beings to vastly increase the sensation of strength while vastly reducing the sensation of effort. It is *both of these together* that define the superpower zone. A world-class weight lifter is physically powerful, but anyone can see that performing an Olympic dead lift requires tremendous physical, mental, and even emotional strain, prepared for by years of training. Someone operating even the most ordinary forklift, on the other hand, can not only lift far more weight than any athlete but can do it with almost no exertion at all.

So superpowers are not just super powerful but also super easy. The superheroes of the classic comic-book era—Superman, Spider-Man, Wonder Woman—could fly, climb skyscrapers, and outrace freight trains without breaking a sweat.

At first, our successful attempts at superpowers granted us superhuman strength—the core achievement of the industrial revolution of the nineteenth century, initially powered by steam and then accelerated by the harnessing of hydrocarbons. But then we naturally began to seek the same kind of effortless power in other dimensions of being human. Especially, in the information revolution of the twentieth century, the mind. Simple mathematics like multiplication and division used to require mental effort, but now anyone who knows how to use a calculator can compute square roots and logarithms with the flick of a finger. Celebrated figures of the past would construct elaborate "memory palaces" to increase their powers of recall. Now the gates of humanity's collective memory palace are wide open to anyone with a search bar in their browser.

The defining superpower of the moment, social media, goes to the very core of our human design, our design for love. Social media has given almost everyone a taste of the kind of recognition and affirmation that used to be available only to a handful of movie stars and television personalities. From Myspace to Facebook to Instagram to the latest app on your fifteen-year-old neighbor's home screen, a series of platforms have granted us low-friction relationships, along with highly visible cues of our status and standing with others. They have given us recognition and influence at a distance: social superpowers.

I started seriously thinking about superpowers around 2012, when I was reporting a story in Silicon Valley. One of the principal subjects was Sonny Vu, whose company Misfit had just launched a line of elegant wearable fitness trackers. Vu is the very embodiment of a tech entrepreneur. He named the company after one of Apple's most famous advertisements ("Here's to the crazy ones. The misfits. The rebels. The troublemakers . . ."). On the day I visited, he was dressed in a black T-shirt and jeans, an outfit that could have come straight from Steve Jobs's closet.

"People want superpowers," Vu told me, when I asked what he thought was most significant about the technology he was developing. "We aspire to extend our capacities, to be better—wearable technology can help us achieve that. We also want to account for our weaknesses, to correct bad habits. Wearable technology can help do that too."

Since I met Sonny Vu, "superpowers" has become a common, almost inescapable, way of describing the potential benefits of new tech. The founder of a coding academy announced confidently in a blog post, "Coding gives you superpowers!" I downloaded a new application for online meetings and discovered, sure enough, that it wanted to give me "presenting superpowers." And not long after I spoke with Vu, *Fast Company* magazine featured an article that could have been taken straight from his pitch deck: "4 Wearables That Give You Superpowers." The subtitle doubled down on the "super" theme: "Super strength. Super hearing. Super artistry. Super expression. The future of wearables is really a quest for human enhancement."

We are obsessed with this quest, whether we're conscious of it or not. Yet when you look at what happens when we acquire these superpowers, it's striking not just how much they add to our capacity but how much they inevitably end up taking away.

Here is the problem: You cannot take advantage of a superpower and fully remain a person, in the sense of a heart-soul-mind-strength complex designed for love. This is not an unfortunate side effect of superpowers or a flaw that could be overcome with future improvements. It is the essence of their design because superpowers are *power without effort*. And power without effort, it turns out, diminishes us as much as it delights us.

Power without effort requires a trade, or a bargain, of sorts: You get superpowers, all right, but only part of you gets to come along for the ride.

Picture yourself flying on a commercial aircraft, traveling without the slightest exertion from one place to another, at such high speeds that for all practical purposes, you might be experiencing the teleportation of science fiction—for what does it really matter if it takes minutes or hours to traverse a continent or an ocean? It's a superpower.

But in order to have this experience, you must be willing to put essential parts of yourself on hold. The first thing that has to go (and this is no accident, but absolutely essential to the superpower dream) is the final term of the Shema's inventory of "alls": your muchness, your strength.

Your body is designed for movement, but for the duration of the flight you will be expected to be unnaturally still (not to mention, at least in economy class, effectively confined to a tiny amount of space). Your senses are dulled too. If you were to make the same journey of hundreds or thousands of miles by horse, bicycle, or sailboat—all of them nonsuperpower modes of transport—those senses would be alive like few other times in your life, calling forth emotional, intellectual, and even spiritual response at the sight of mountains, the sharp snap of cold air, the bite of the wind, the brilliance of the stars. You would be living the "muchness" that is the full meaning of that Hebrew word *me'od*.

Instead, on this journey your senses recede. Among the first to go at high altitude is taste, which is why the flavors of airline food and drink are made deliberately simple. Your mind, too, feels like it is slowly turning to mush, even before you distract yourself by turning on the romantic comedy offered by the in-flight entertainment system. It's a movie you would never consent to watch in any other circumstance, but somehow now it is strangely appealing.

With enough money, flying can become a tolerable experience—a larger seat in which to sit doing nothing, a larger screen through which to consume entertainment, a larger tray table on which will be placed more elaborately prepared bland food. But no matter how pleasant, the fundamental experience offered by airplane flight is the very opposite of strength, of muchness, of *me'od*. To be borne aloft by the extraordinary power of a jet engine requires you to set aside most of your heart, soul, mind, and strength for the duration of the flight.

Now, the experiences we have once we disembark may well bring us back to the fullness for which we are designed. We return to family and friends at holidays to see one another face to face, to sit down at a feast, to embrace and converse. We travel to distant countries where we have heard that the scenery is spectacular and the food enlivening. But the travel *itself* undermines rather than supplements this experience—indeed, for hours or days after getting off the plane, we may feel out of place in body, mind, and heart, struggling to connect with a new place and the people in it. And the very hunger for travel is driven in part by the flattened nature of our daily lives, the rarity of genuine, solid heart-soul-mind-strength love in our superpower-seeking world.

PEAK PERFORMANCE

To be sure, the superpower zone does not always feel as passive as air travel has become. Indeed, it can be exhilarating—as it is when I floor the accelerator in my car or, for that matter, open up my notifications and swipe them away, one after another, with the flick of a finger. In these moments, our experience of the superpower zone resembles the times of peak performance—fully present, fully engaged, acting decisively and creatively, with focus and energy—that the psychologist Mihaly Csikszentmihalyi popularized years ago as "flow."

I am no world-class cyclist, but for me, there is no

more reliable way to enter flow than on my bicycle. Most afternoons, during the pleasant months of the year, I take a twenty-mile ride that loops through a local state park. Though I enjoy the rush of air, the changing scenery, and the subtle scents of a Pennsylvania spring, summer, or fall, this is not a pleasure ride. A smartphone is mounted on my bike handlebars, allowing me to track my pace and cadence against past rides and push myself to greater speed and efficiency of movement. I feel the effort in burning muscles, intense gulps of air, and the pounding of my heart.

I get on my bike in any number of different moods, some days with a sense of energy and optimism, many other days weighed down by fatigue or depression. But when I get off twenty miles later, I am almost always in roughly the same mood: grateful, calm, and alert (and also, of course, ready for a shower). I've experienced at least some measure of flow.

The superpower zone, at its most beguiling, comes close to simulating this experience, which is why so much of consumer spending is devoted to its pursuit. We buy a drone so we can vicariously fly; we buy headphones so we can be immersed in sound. We open up a news feed in our browser and find ourselves drawn in to novelty, amusement, or outrage served up at whatever pace our appetite desires. But what we are experiencing in these moments is quite different from flow—most clearly in the way they begin and the way they end.

The superpower zone begins with a sensation of

rushing power, excitement, and anticipation. Our most godlike abilities are about to be unleashed; our nagging anxieties are about to recede. Often we feel a delightful sense of accomplishment even before anything has really happened—a surge of pleasure, for example, as the familiar title sequence of our current Netflix series begins to play.

Flow, on the other hand, has no such reliable pattern. Indeed, because the way into it is generally through significant creative effort or physical exertion, we may actually enter the work with resistance or apprehension. No one knows this better than writers and artists, who know the dread that can accompany sitting down to any creative task. Often flow simply begins, as with my daily bike rides, with whatever emotional state we carry into the experience. At the beginning we may feel that nothing is changing—indeed it is very possible that we will not even notice as our mood begins to shift.

And what about the ending? When flow subsides, as it inevitably does, we are left with a sense of gratitude, humility, and even awe. We feel strangely okay. In that moment, we are able to trust that the next time we need to concentrate and perform at a high level, that ability will mysteriously be there once again. Even though we have just engaged in a kind of profound fullness, we are newly at ease with emptiness, with being our small, ordinary selves. We are open to other people, perhaps even to God and the cosmos, in a new way.

Exiting the superpower zone is a very different experience. For one thing, we rarely do so willingly. Just watch a ten-year-old called away from his video game to the family meal. He has been immersed in a world of super-powers, of lightning-fast reflexes and capacity for action. For a time he has had the abilities of an NFL quarterback or a Navy SEAL in combat—now it's time to be a ten-year-old again. No wonder he dithers and delays, up to the point of defiant fury. (There is, after all, no dinner hour in the superpower zone.)

And yet, for all the ways we cling to the superpower zone as we are dragged off by a parent, spouse, or other responsibilities, when we look back from a distance, our memories of our time spent there are strangely inert. If we can remember the experience at all, it seems that we were in some kind of alternate universe that cannot really touch or inform our own—which in fact is precisely true. We have none of the rich, grateful memories that we do of our moments of real flow. We can recall, perhaps, that we were feeling pleasure and potency, but the pleasure and potency themselves are absent. All that is left is a hollow sense of loss.

And there's another catch: Any given superpower de-livers its initial rush of excitement only the first few times we encounter it. Over time, that excitement diminishes.

In its early decades, air travel, with all its passive lux-ury, was an exhilarating experience, but it has dwindled into tedium. Perhaps you dream of becoming a regular traveler by private jet, but should that happen to you, the same exact pattern will play out: The first few trips will be

thrilling and you will hardly be able to resist taking out
your smartphone to document the moment. Over time,
though, travel by private jet subsides just as completely as
commercial air travel to a distant, dull roar.

Flow, on the other hand, does not seem to subside
in the same way. I experience just as much serenity and
joy on my bike today—maybe more—as I did on my first
long rides as a teenager nearly forty years ago. Though
it cannot be coerced or captured, flow is mysteriously,
graciously renewed over the course of our lives.

Flow is the timelessness of a live performance, the
moments when the skill and vulnerability of the artist in
the presence of an audience somehow hold in reverent
suspension all we have known and dreamed of life. The
superpower zone is clicking on the double arrow that will
start the fifth episode in a row of *The Office*.

Flow is the tenth mile of the New York City Marathon, when you're cheered on by crowds and building on
all your training to find a pace right at the edge of your
ability. The superpower zone is walking while texting on
a New York City sidewalk.

Flow is that conversation with someone who might
become your beloved, where a spark of mutual interest
kindles a fast-moving exchange of words and emotion,
eye contact held and broken over and over. The superpower zone is swiping over and over on Tinder—an activity that its users perform, according to the company,
an average of eighty to ninety minutes per day.

Flow is a taste of eternity, where even time itself will

be caught up into a widening gyre of grace. The super-power zone, spiraling into malaise and addiction, is a taste of hell.

FLEETING PLEASURES

In recent years, we have learned much more about why our newfound superpowers are so rewarding in the short term—and in the long term, so diminishing.

Our most basic bodily system for experiencing reward is the dopamine system, which floods our bodies with a sense of pleasure and satisfaction. It is one of the most basic motivators in human experience—indeed, almost all our motivation is felt at the bodily level because of the influence of dopamine. No aspect of our lives can be reduced to the merely electrical or chemical, but because we are so thoroughly embodied as persons, every aspect of our lives is reflected in and mediated by these remarkable and delicate systems.

Most of us are aware of the finding, summarized by the eminent University of Cambridge neuroscientist Wolfram Schultz in a 2016 paper, that "drugs of addiction," like "cocaine, amphetamine, methamphetamine, nicotine, and alcohol . . . generate, hijack, and amplify the dopamine reward signal." But the real power of these drugs goes beyond their ability to generate rewards. As Schultz and his collaborators have demonstrated, in work that earned him the prestigious Gruber Neuroscience

Prize, not only do these drugs unleash floods of rewarding dopamine, but they also prevent us from learning that their rewards are fleeting. By interfering with "reward prediction," the most powerful hijackers of the dopamine pathway create the sensation, at a primal level of our brains, that their rewards are ever new and ever worth pursuing—even as our own self-awareness and reflection tell us they are damaging and degrading.

This is the shadow side, Schultz has shown, of the beneficial function of the dopamine system, which is not just to deliver hits of satisfaction but to help the brain learn what actually contributes to health and well-being. We are built to learn over time what produces real reward—we are designed with built-in systems to help us anticipate, and pursue, the good. But in the era of superpowers, we have developed ever more powerful ways around this system. Alcohol and nicotine, along with a handful of other intoxicants discovered by premodern people, were one of the original pathways to a sensation of superpowers—but the other items in Schultz's list are what we call drugs. Cocaine and meth, as well as the high-potency cannabis now available in lozenges and "edibles," are not merely the by-product of fermentation or the cultivation of a particular plant but technologically engineered substances designed to maximize the sensation of superpower reward.

And while nothing can quite match drugs for their ability to directly plug into and hijack our most basic neurological pathways, it turns out that everything from gambling to social media can grant us the same super-power sensation—and create the same learning-resistant illusion. Though I'm not sure anyone has ever studied the neuroscience of car acceleration, this certainly would explain why, though I know that the stop sign on my street is just a block away, I still press down on the accelerator pedal, reaping the unearned reward of speed. On a bicycle, where every increase in speed requires an increase in exertion, I would quickly learn to coast to a halt rather than waste energy in that way.

But when the next hit of dopamine is just a button away, neither brain nor body has a reason to stop and ask whether we are growing or diminishing, thriving or dwindling. There is one thing you don't do in the super-power zone, it turns out: You never really learn.

ASKING LESS OF OURSELVES

Steve Myrland has worked with some of the best-developed athletes in the world. Years ago he served as a strength-and-conditioning coach at the University of Wisconsin, training rowers, tennis players, cross-country runners, and national championship teams in other sports; later, as a coach with the National Hockey League San Jose Sharks, he contributed to record-setting improvements in the team's performance. I met him a few years later through my friend Robert Kehoe, a writer who was rising before dawn three times a week to join Myrland

and a few dozen other men and women in a high school field house. These early morning training sessions have become somewhat legendary in the city of Madison. Kehoe thought Myrland had some insights that would help me understand what has happened to our bodies in the technological era, and indeed he did.

Myrland's most basic insight, the one that has shaped much of his training philosophy, is the importance of the three dimensions of human movement. We not only move in straight lines up and down, forward and back, and side to side (along what are called the sagittal and frontal planes). We also translate energy through the transverse plane, an imaginary horizontal division through the middle of our body, using the "core" muscles that rotate and transmit torque as we walk, run, swim, or even crawl. Effective athletic conditioning, Myrland has come to believe, involves all these dimensions rather than just one or two. And yet he has discovered that even elite athletes often fail to train in all three planes of motion.

"I can walk into a room of alumni of the rowing team, even decades after they graduated," he tells me, "and tell immediately which side each one rowed on"—because their bodies are unnaturally developed on one side and underdeveloped on the other. "If you only train the body in one dimension, it will adapt. But an *adapted* body is not an *adaptable* body, one that can move with strength and agility in any direction. And that means that an adapted body is more susceptible to injury and never reaches its full potential."

The worst thing that ever happened to athletic training, in Myrland's view, was the invention of fitness
machines—the devices that fill gyms all over the world.
By isolating muscles and compelling them to move in
just one plane of motion, fitness machines ask our bodies
to do something they were never meant to do. Bodies
trained on these machines do adapt to the training—put
in enough reps on a biceps machine, and that single set
of muscles will develop—but at the price of becoming
fundamentally less fit overall.

So, instead of using machines that isolate parts of the
body, Myrland says, "We train on our feet." His work-
outs involve little equipment. Instead, they often rely on
intensive person-to-person cooperation. Myrland hands
me one end of a six-foot length of rigid PVC pipe and
grabs the other end. We face each other, holding it over
our shoulders javelin style. "Now give me some resistance," he says. I lean forward, putting my weight into
the bar, as Myrland pushes back. It's a kind of reverse
tug-of-war, an exercise not just in strength and balance
but also communication, as we continually adjust our effort to match the force the other person is putting in.
And though the tube itself weighs a few pounds at most,
the exercise is as challenging as you want to make it—
because someone else is pushing back on the other end
with their own strength.

In the months after my meeting with Myrland, I start
asking friends and groups to whom I speak a simple question: How much of your day is spent in activities that ask

you to move and torque your body in all three anatomi-
cal planes?

The pattern, of course, is predictable. When I am
with people who work in the trades—carpenters, plumb-
ers, the masons who rebuilt the stone patio outside our
house—I'm with three-plane people. When I am with
people who do the work of childcare or elder care, there
is plenty of three-plane activity—as any parent of a toddler or an adult child of aging parents can attest. Indeed,
work that was labeled "essential" during the COVID-19
lockdowns involved three-plane activity.

But much of the time, I am surrounded by people like
me, whose work takes place in front of a screen or perhaps around conference tables or in front of a classroom.
And our daily life in the body requires, well, no planes.

Myrland's insights are true at the most basic level of
strength conditioning, but they are also the key to understanding so much of our diminished life. Just as a
rower who always rows on the left side will end up with
an adapted body that can no longer distribute strength
evenly, so we, who were meant to live with an allness of
heart, soul, mind, and strength, have gradually atrophied
in the crucial dimensions of personhood.

We have adapted, as human beings do, to the presence of superpowers, but we are underdeveloped in so
many ways—and, like those overly adapted bodies, terribly susceptible to injury. We flatter ourselves that we
live in a "developed" world—but it is an adapted world,
a lopsided world. And it is a lonely world because the

one thing that you cannot enhance, supercharge, or out-source in human life is the one thing we most need: the patient process of search and recognition, absence and return, rupture and repair that adds up to being known.

Over time, the active verbs of the Shema—*recite, walk, talk, lie down, rise, bind, fix, write,* all in the service of *love*—become too much for us to imagine, let alone perform.

Our search for superpowers has created many of the most pressing problems of our time.

The defining mental activity of our time is scrolling. Our capacities of attention, memory, and concentration are diminishing; to compensate, we toggle back and forth between infinite feeds of news, posts, images, episodes—taking shallow hits of trivia, humor, and outrage to make up for the depths of learning, joy, and genuine lament that now feel beyond our reach.

The defining illness of our time is metabolic syndrome, the chronic combination of high weight, high cholesterol, high blood pressure, and high blood sugar that is the hallmark of an inactive life. Our strength is atrophying and our waistline expanding, and to compensate, we turn to the superpowers of the supermarket, with the aisles of salt and fat convincing our bodies' reward systems, one bite at a time, that we have never been better in our life.

The defining emotional challenge of our time is anxiety, the fear of what might be instead of the courageous pursuit of what could be. Once, we lived with allness of heart, with a boldness of quest that was too in love with the good to call off the pursuit when we encountered risk. Now we live as voyeurs, pursuing shadowy vestiges of what we desire from behind the one-way mirror of a screen, invulnerable but alone.

And, of course, the soul is the plane of human existence that our technological age neglects most of all. Jesus asked whether it was worth gaining the whole world at the cost of losing one's soul. But in the era of superpowers, we have not only lost a great deal of our souls—we have lost much of the world as well. We are rarely overwhelmed by wind or rain or snow. We rarely see, let alone name, the stars. We have lost the sense that we are both at home and on a pilgrimage in the vast, mysterious cosmos, anchored in a rich reality beyond ourselves. We have lost our souls without even gaining the world.

So it is no wonder that the defining condition of our time is a sense of loneliness and alienation.

For if human flourishing requires us to love with all our hearts, souls, minds, and strength, what happens when nothing in our lives develops those capacities? With what, exactly, will we love?

MODERN MAGIC

The Ancient Roots of Our Tech Obsession

How did we end up with a world so poorly designed for human beings—so poorly designed for our hearts, souls, minds, and strength?

The answer lies in a fairy tale—but unlike the fairy tales we tell to children, this is one that some of the smartest people in the world have believed in, dreamed of, and tried to build. The harder we have tried to build it, the more impersonal our world has become, because the dream is based on a lie.

The dream is that human beings could acquire the ultimate superpower: the ability to do magic.

We no longer call it by that name, to be sure. Instead, we call it technology. But as the science fiction author Arthur C. Clarke famously observed, "Any sufficiently advanced technology is indistinguishable from magic." The quality that delights and intoxicates us in our technological devices is the way they promise to work without us, without asking very much of us—like magic. But what this quest for magic ultimately does to us, and through us, is make the world uninhabitable for persons.

Our desire for magic has a long history—as long and as universal, in some ways, as the human story itself. But it is woven especially into the story of what we often call the West—the European and then North American societies that pursued technology most avidly even as they built an economy to maximize its potential and apparent returns.

The problem is not just that magic doesn't work. The problem is not even, as I will argue later, that technology, for all its real benefits, will never work in the magical way we are constantly being told that it soon will. The problem is what we do when our quest for impersonal power is frustrated. It turns out that this dream is so strong that we are quite willing to press persons into service, treating them more like things and machines than like human beings, rather than see the dream die.

If magic worked—and we have told ourselves, over and over, how we might get it to work—it could set everyone free. But because magic does not work, our quest for its replacement will ultimately make everyone a slave. That's why our world feels so inhospitable to persons—why the world even of the relatively powerful, let alone the relatively powerless, feels so compulsive so much of the time.

Remarkably, all these themes are present in one of

those fairy tales I mentioned earlier. It was first committed to writing just as modern science was beginning to emerge from the medieval practice of alchemy. It's a superficially charming story that anticipates everything that can go wrong when we pursue the magic our devices promise. And this tale came to be told with one of the most recognizable characters in the world in its starring role: Mickey Mouse, playing the sorcerer's apprentice.

HAT TRICK

Johann Wolfgang von Goethe's ballad "Der Zauberlehrling" ("The Sorcerer's Apprentice"), written in 1797, might hardly be remembered today if a French composer named Paul Dukas had not composed a symphonic poem in tribute to it exactly one hundred years later. His music was, in turn, picked up by the animators of Walt Disney Studios. They made Goethe's brief tale, set to Dukas's memorable music, the centerpiece of the groundbreaking 1940 film *Fantasia*.

In Disney's version, Mickey Mouse commandeers the sorcerer's magic hat after his master has gone to bed. It quickly occurs to him to use his new magical powers to summon a broom in the corner, making it take over the job of fetching water to fill the basin in the magician's tower.

Elated with his new freedom from toil—deep in the superpower zone, we might say—Mickey falls asleep, dreaming of ever more fantastical exercises of magical power. As the music swells, he soars in his dream into the heavens, where his magic commands the stars. But he is rudely awakened by the discovery that the magic broom has taken its assignment far too literally, continuing to bring buckets of water long after the basin is filled. When Mickey attempts to chop it into bits with an ax, each piece becomes its own monomaniacal broom. Only at the last moment is the apprentice saved from drowning by the return of the sorcerer, who banishes the magical brooms and sends his apprentice back to his lowly task with a swift smack on the backside.

It is easy enough, especially when the tale comes in the form of a Disney cartoon, to treat the misadventures of the sorcerer's apprentice as a story with a moral no more complex than "Be careful what you wish for"— much as the Disney version of the tale of Aladdin turns the remorseless Jinn of *The Arabian Nights* into a wise-cracking and good-natured sidekick.

Mickey Mouse, with his button eyes and his sheepish grin, is the way we like to see ourselves and our relationship to technology· essentially innocent, simply looking for a bit of relief from the drudgery of our lives, at worst tempted by our devices the way that children are tempted by cookies in a jar on the shelf.

But what if apprenticing to a sorcerer is not such a great idea in the first place? Perhaps this is the kind of internship you shouldn't be too eager to accept. What if the sorcerer, whose magic hat we yearn to wear and

wield, gained his powers at a price that never should have
been paid?

THE ALCHEMISTS' DREAM

Before there was technology, there was alchemy.

For centuries, alchemy was the preoccupation of the
greatest minds of Europe, which had imported its fundamental principles and practices from India and the Is-
lamic world (which gave it the Arabic name *al-kimiya*).
Figures now remembered for other contributions—the
physician Paracelsus, the astronomer Tycho Brahe, and
the physicist Isaac Newton—in fact devoted most of their
energies to alchemy in its various forms.

Some of the alchemists' work was a kind of folk science, and they had discovered various useful properties
of natural substances ranging from metals to plants. But
the alchemists were also lured, or driven, by what they
called the *magnum opus,* or "great work," which centered
on the quest for a substance called the philosopher's
stone—a substance that, if it could be discovered or produced, would turn base metals into gold.

You might think that alchemy would have entirely dis-
appeared in our scientific age. After all, we're told, the
alchemists' experiments didn't work (and weren't even
properly experiments). It was modern science that truly
unlocked the secrets of nature. The alchemists failed; the
chemists succeeded.

It is odd, then, how frequently alchemy continues to show up in popular culture, very much in plain sight. Paolo Coelho's fable *The Alchemist* has sold 150 million copies. (Somehow it's hard to imagine a novel called *The Chemist* doing the same.) And then, of course, there's the lead-off book in the bestselling series of novels of all time, with the philosopher's stone right there in the title—though it was changed, for the American market, to the "Sorcerer's Stone."

Alchemy did fail in the simplest sense—no philosopher's stone was ever found and none ever will be. But in another sense, alchemy succeeded. It gave us a dream—along with the belief that the dream is tantalizingly close to being within our grasp. It felt to the alchemists, and still feels to us today, just out of reach, just around the corner, one breakthrough away.

What was this dream? First and most fundamentally, the alchemists believed that there was a magical power locked within the natural world—one that, if unlocked, would transform human existence. This power was hidden and esoteric, a secret tucked away in nature that only the erudite and elect could fathom.

Second, the essential work of the alchemist was to distill and purify the elements of the world in such a way that they were gradually transformed into the most pure and powerful substance, gold.

Third, this metallurgical transformation (in which all metals could ultimately be transmuted into gold) was just the beginning. It was the prelude to a spiritual transformation of humanity. Just as metal was gradually freed of its impurities, so, too, the successful alchemist could be liberated from the impurity of embodied existence, set free from toil, and elevated to the status of a god. Having gone through this transformation, one would attain immortal life, the kind of life available only to a purely spiritual being.

The alchemists considered themselves to be performing magic—not in the sense of impressive or charming tricks, but in the sense of unlocking and acquiring the ability to command nature. The word *command* is essential. Magic is not essentially about *understanding* the world, especially if we note that word's humble implication that true knowledge involves "standing under" something. Magic is about standing over, not under. At the heart of magic is the belief that, given the right code words—"abracadabra" being the schoolchild's imitation of the magician's incantation—a human being can gain unquestioned control of the forces at the heart of the cosmos.

The more circumspect alchemists never claimed that they would become God "with a capital *G*," as we might say, but they were not shy about aspiring to a divine role. Carl Jung, hardly a traditional Christian, studied the alchemists carefully and believed they courted serious spiritual danger with dictums like this one, from the physician Paracelsus: "I under the Lord, the Lord under me, I under him outside my office, and he under me outside his office." In the words of one of Paracelsus's contemporaries, which Jung also quoted with disapproval, the alchemist saw himself as being "philosopher, demon, hero, God, and all things."

When Yuval Harari, the popular historian who is celebrated by technological elites, titled his bestselling book *Homo Deus: A Brief History of Tomorrow*, he was directly invoking the core dream of the alchemists—that by the acquisition of magical powers rooted in the very nature of the cosmos, human beings would take their place alongside, or altogether take the place of, God.

There was, of course, a catch. Actually getting hold of those magic forces, and getting them to do what you wanted, turned out to be a devilishly difficult business. The alchemists' notebooks do not read like the disciplined, patient experimental records of Michael Faraday or Marie Curie, which converge on simple and elegant findings. Instead, they evoke the half-crazed excitement of a conspiracy theorist who believes he is just about to find the final link in an incredibly complex web of associations. The effortless power of magic kept slipping through their grasp.

So the alchemists generally concluded, after much frustrated experimentation, that they could not work their magic independently after all. Perhaps they needed assistance—they needed to be able to summon some entity with extra insight into the magic forces they were trying to harness. Thus, they sought out the aid of a "familiar spirit," uttering various spells and prayers, to enlist supernatural assistance in their quest for mastery of the world.

But it turns out that the spirits summoned by such

methods are, like Mickey's broom, not always inclined to follow orders. Or, as Goethe put it, in words that every German speaker knows by heart, *Die ich rief, die Geister, / Werd ich nun nicht los.* "The spirits which I have summoned / I now cannot banish."

The quest for magic does, after all, lead to encountering a kind of power—but it is one that masters us, not the other way around.

IMPERSONAL MAGIC

If there is one belief that defines modern people, it is the belief that magic, whether of the shaman, the sorcerer, or the alchemist, does not really exist. We "know" that the world is merely material rather than also spiritual, that it operates impersonally rather than personally, that whatever the world is able to give us by way of abundance and possibility will be achieved not by conjuring and magic but by calculation and mechanism.

Our society has taken a strange turn from the magic to which the alchemists were devoted—along with sorcerers and wonder workers in all kinds of cultures throughout history. But, in fact, the old, traditional, personal kind of magic and the new, modern, impersonal kind are linked. They trace back to the same source, and they actually end up in the same place. The alchemists, after all, were not looking for genuine partners, a genuine other to be their companions in unlocking the secrets of the world.

Instead, they assumed that the spirits they summoned could be commanded and coerced. When Mary Shelley's Dr. Frankenstein discovers that his monster yearns for companionship and love, he drives him away in horror. The sorcerer's apprentice wants a magical broom, but he does not want something (let alone someone) with dignity and a will of its own—he wants not just a servant but a slave.

This puts a more sinister light on Arthur C. Clarke's claim about technology being indistinguishable from magic. It is amazing how often Clarke's dictum is quoted with unironic reverence, as a genuine guide to the direction that the human race should go. In fact, anyone who really understood the distorting history of magic—its tendency to displace God, its quest to enslave nature, its recurring obsession with fashioning beings to serve the magician, and above all its stunningly consistent failure to actually deliver on its promises—would hope that a sufficiently advanced technology would be *very readily distinguishable from magic.*

Unlike magic, a truly advanced technology should make us more fully persons, not less, the longer we use it. It should connect us ever more deeply to other people, to nature, and to God; should be of special benefit to the vulnerable, not just solving their problems but elevating their dignity; and should have increasing benefits even for those who do not wield it, rather than degrading everyone but the ones who possess it.

By this measure, we do not seem at all to be head-ing in the direction of a sufficiently advanced technology. Or, perhaps, we have exactly fulfilled Clarke's—and the alchemists'—vision. We are managing to do magic, but it turns out that the quest for impersonal power ultimately puts us at the mercy of something worse than boredom or loneliness.

And this brings us to the ultimate source of impersonal power in our world, the driving motive behind modern technology. It is the power, Jesus taught, that competes most single-mindedly with the God who made us for worship of him and love for one another. It is this power above all, I believe, that lured the alchemists and also drove them mad. It is the one thing Jesus of Nazareth explicitly said you could not serve while also serving God—and to underscore his point, Jesus gave this malign force a distinctive and singular name.

This spirit, once summoned, turns out to be very hard to banish indeed.

MONEY AND MAMMON

How Impersonal Power Rules Our World

They say that a friend is "someone who will help you move." They also say a *true* friend is "someone who will help you move . . . a body," though I have never had a chance to experience that level of friendship.

Several friends helped Catherine and me move into our first apartment, down and then up two steep and narrow sets of stairs. Three items seemed almost impossible to get up those stairs: a fragile old chest of drawers my wife had inherited from her grandmother, a queen-sized box spring, and an unfathomably heavy sofa bed. We christened them the Ordeal of Delicacy, the Ordeal of Dimension, and the Ordeal of Strength. Twenty years later, we remember those ordeals; the friends who cheerfully endured them with us, sweating and swearing on a hot June day; and the sense of relief when we managed to overcome each one.

A few years later, it was time to move again when my wife took the job she has held ever since. This time, the college that hired her covered the moving costs. The professional movers went through the same ordeals on our behalf that our friends had gone through a few years before—sweating and likely swearing as well—but I certainly cannot remember their names, nor even a hint of their faces. They were paid, fairly, to do a fair job. And once the job was done, they were gone.

This is the power of money: It allows us to get things done, often by means of other persons, without the entanglements of friendship.

To this day, I owe my friends something for the move early in our marriage—at the very least, my thanks and my affection. Indeed, I already owed them something before the move. To be a friend is to be intertwined with someone else in a loose but permanent way. Friendships can fade—I have fallen out of touch with at least one of the people who helped us move that day, and based on what I know, our lives have gone in very different directions. And yet I could never say that that person is not my friend. Thinking of that person today brings up a sense of unfinished obligation and possibility that time and distance have made only more bittersweet.

But our relationship, such as it was, with the professional movers was different. It began and ended with a modern form of magic—a transaction that, without the

slightest actual effort on our part, transported all our pos-
sessions from Boston to Philadelphia and set them down,
unharmed, in our new home. The moment the movers
placed the last box in our living room and departed, our
dependence on them was at an end. The experience was
relationally weightless, imposing no burden and leaving
no trace.

The distinctive thing that money allows us—its most
seductive promise—is abundance without dependence.

The alchemists dreamed of turning every metal into
gold—for most of history the most valuable and reliable
form of currency. Someone who was able to turn metal
into gold would be endlessly able to work the magic that
only money can do: to induce others to provide for our
needs and satisfy our wants, with no reciprocity or loyalty
required.

For the more we enter the money economy, the less
personal our world becomes. When we were infants and
had no money, any good that came into our lives came
from persons who loved us—most often because they
were related to us—and cared for us without expecting
any return other than our love in response. But today, we
can make a dozen purchases in a day and never learn the
name of a single person who produces, sells, or delivers
what we buy.

Money has contributed, genuinely, to human flourishing. It has facilitated the extraordinary exchange
of value unlocked by the industrial and computational
revolutions. A good job well done and fairly paid—as

I believe was the case for the men who helped in our move—contributes to human dignity and the common good.

But money has not helped us to be persons. It operates in a sphere where heart-soul-mind-strength complexes designed for love are simply not relevant. It is designed for a world where we do not need love, or even relationship, to get what we want. The more time we spend in the world that money makes, the more we become conformed to its image.

Money is the culmination, and the engine, of a world of impersonal power. If I have money—and almost everything in the modern world depends on that *if*—I can live the dream of the sorcerer's apprentice, or indeed the sorcerer himself, conjuring up the goods and services I require and desire without entangling myself with the personalities and needs of other people. If I cannot yet turn anything into gold, at least I can turn my money into almost anything I want. Whatever you desire in this world, there is almost certainly someone who, whether legally or not, will find a way to give it to you—if you have money. And money is one thing our world has more of than it has ever had.

It all works astonishingly like magic—with the lightness of being that was the alchemists' dream.

WHAT MAMMON WANTS

There is a name for this global system, the system that powers and is powered by the technological magic we all wield to some extent on a daily basis. It is an ancient name, and I have come to believe it is best understood as a proper name—that is, not just a generic noun, but a name for someone.

The name is Mammon.

We encounter this name in one of Jesus' most stark and unsettling pronouncements, rendered this way by the King James Version: "Ye cannot serve God and mammon" (Matt. 6:24). In speaking about the danger of earthly treasure in the Sermon on the Mount, Jesus describes Mammon as a rival to God, an alternative lord. *Mammon* is an Aramaic word, and the apostles who preserved Jesus' teachings generally translated them from Aramaic into the Greek their readers knew best. They could easily have done so with *Mammon,* using words for "money" or even "wealth" that have little negative connotation. Instead, they left this Aramaic word untranslated, suggesting that it had particular significance.

By the first centuries of the Christian church, teachers and bishops had concluded that in using the name *Mammon,* Jesus had in mind not just a concept but a demonic power. Money, for Jesus, was not a neutral tool but something that could master a person every bit as completely as the true God. Mammon is not simply money but the anti-God impetus that finds its power in money.

And the more we understand the distorting power of Mammon in the human story, the more it does seem to take on a will of its own. *What Technology Wants,* the title of the 2010 book by Kevin Kelly, seems like a slightly exaggerated rhetorical flourish—but a book called *What Mammon Wants* would have an enormous and terrifying plausibility.

For Mammon does want something very much indeed, because Mammon is ultimately not at all just a thing, nor even a system, but a will at work in history. And what it wants, above all, is to separate power from relationship, abundance from dependence, and being from personhood.

This is why technology, adopted with such enthusiasm for its potential for human flourishing, so often seems to go strangely off the rails. As the Christian theologian Craig Gay perceptively observes in his book *Modern Technology and the Human Future,* technology does not exist primarily, and never existed primarily, to serve us or support "ordinary embodied human existence." Rather, Gay argues, it has always been developed to serve first and foremost the generation of economic profit—*whether or not* it also contributes to real, personal flourishing.

This is a subtle but important point. In many cases technology does truly bring good into our lives. Hospitals use automated infusion pumps to administer precise doses of medicine according to a rigorous schedule, relieving human beings of a task that even the most dedicated nurses would find hard to perform consistently.

When such benefit for human beings aligns with economic profit, technology "wants" it.

But technology also "wants" things that do *not* confer any net benefit on human beings other than the owners of technology companies. The insurance company that pays for infusion pumps can also gather medical data, divorced both from human context and human responsibility, in order to make more profitable decisions about what conditions—and perhaps eventually what individuals—they refuse to insure. While these impulses are reined in to some extent by regulation, there is no doubt that left to their own devices, the companies that deploy technology "want" this outcome too.

Sometimes the results are mixed. Human beings may well benefit, for example, by having access to unlimited amounts of recorded music from all over the world and from the whole history of recorded music. Sure enough, technology is glad to provide that—at an economic profit to the owners of streaming services, although not in a way that sustains more than a handful of actual working human musicians.

But human beings also benefit enormously from *making* music, which requires deep communal instruction, personal attention, and years of practice and preparation. This, alas, is a kind of benefit technology cannot readily provide—at least not profitably—so technology does not particularly "want" to help. So we end up with the world we have, where more music is consumed than ever and less music is created, especially by ordinary people in economically sustainable ways, than ever.

What technology wants is really what Mammon wants: a world of context-free, responsibility-free, dependence-free power measured out in fungible, storable units of value. And ultimately what Mammon wants is to turn a world made for and stewarded by persons into a world made of and reduced to things.

Thus, the reason for Jesus' stark statement about God and Mammon becomes clear. We cannot serve the true God and Mammon, ultimately, because their aims are precisely opposed to each other. God wishes to put all things into the service of persons and ultimately to bring forth the flourishing of creation through the flourishing of persons. Mammon wants to put all persons into the service of things and ultimately to bring about the exploitation of all of creation.

SUFFICIENTLY ADVANCED TECHNOLOGY

We could have taken a different path at the dawn of the technological era. It was not the alchemists, after all, who taught us how to harness the power available in the created world. It was scientists like James Clerk Maxwell, whose elegant field equations unlocked our understanding of electromagnetic forces. Above the doorway of the Cavendish Laboratory at the University of Cambridge, Maxwell had these words inscribed, a subtle but decisive refusal of the alchemists' dream: *"Magna opera Domini exquisita in omnes voluntates ejus."* That inscription still stands, now in English, above the Laboratory's new building: "The works of the Lord are great, sought out of all them that have pleasure therein" (Ps. 111:2). In Maxwell's lab, the scientist's role was not godlike mastery but humble delight.

If we had refused the alchemists' dream, we could have developed sufficiently advanced technology—sufficiently advanced in that it left behind the dream of magic and refused the service of Mammon.

A sufficiently advanced technology would break loose from the fantasy that we could escape our human condition and become like gods, escape our bodies and their limitations, escape the amazing creative powers of human beings animated by love and acquire superpowers instead. Such technology could still create economic value and increase wealth, but it would never serve the creation of economic value above the flourishing of persons. It would connect us more and more deeply rather than dividing us more and more decisively.

Every time such technology was used, you would have a profound encounter with a person—you would feel reverence for the other as an image bearer, recognizing their face, their name, their story, and their place. Far from thrilling at the sight of things operating on their own with no human effort required, such technology would equip us to see, and rejoice in, the *allness* of human beings pouring their love into works of great emotional resonance, truthfulness and soulfulness, intelligence and insight, strength and dexterity.

We can still turn and take that technological path today.

The research group of MIT Media Lab professor Rosalind Picard has turned out a series of innovations in computation and robotics—innovations that all stem in one way or another from Picard's interest in equipping computers to better interact with human embodiment and, especially, emotion. Among the lab's most consequential inventions is a simple but lifesaving device, approved by the U.S. FDA in 2018, that can be used by persons who suffer from epilepsy. It looks like a smartwatch, and it is sold under the name Embrace.

Epileptic seizures take three thousand lives per year in the United States and fifty thousand lives worldwide. Most epileptic seizures pose a risk of asphyxiation, which can be prevented if someone nearby ensures that the person's airway remains unobstructed and the person is resting in a secure environment. But certain epileptic seizures are so deep that the person's body will shut down altogether for lack of signals from the brain.

It turns out that to be brought back from such a deep suspension, there is one noninvasive intervention that works far better than any other. It can interrupt the misfiring neurons and reestablish normal brain function within a few moments.

Another person needs to speak to you and gently touch you, ideally calling you by name.

This intervention must happen within a matter of minutes in order for the person to survive such a seizure.

This means the only person who can come to the rescue is someone nearby. The Embrace device is designed to alert the nearest person on a list of people the user trusts, ideally including close neighbors. People often cling to their cellphones in case a loved one should call with an emergency—but for this kind of emergency, a cellphone is of no use. Only the nearest person can do anything about it.

It's kind of amazing. Surviving this particular kind of episode is possible if you have a neighbor you trust who will speak to you and touch you and call you by name, activating the same sense of person-to-person recognition that was present at the moment of your birth. It is possible, that is, if you and your neighbor are living a fully *personal* life. If you are willing to know and be known by your neighbors and depend on them at a moment of profound vulnerability, a piece of technology called the Embrace can save your life.

Our future depends on this: whether we decide that we want technology to enable us and our neighbors to be persons for one another.

And should we fail to decide, Mammon knows what Mammon wants—and its preferred future, in far too many ways, is already here.

BORING ROBOTS

Why the Next Tech Revolution Will Succeed—and Also Fail

The word *robot* was first introduced to the world through Karel Čapek's 1921 play, *R.U.R.*, which in English stood for "Rossum's Universal Robots." When we imagine robots today, even humanoid ones, we usually think of them as mechanical things. But the robots in Čapek's play are flesh-and-blood creatures that seem at first glance to be human. In fact, though, they are manufactured, engineered to tirelessly and uncomplainingly perform laborious tasks. By the year 2000, when the play's action begins, they are employed all over the world and are essential to the economy.

The word *robots*, Čapek later wrote, was coined by his brother Josef, drawing on the Slavonic word *robota*. That word means forced labor, or "servitude," a reference to the uncompensated labor serfs performed in the feudal system. The plot of *R.U.R.* involves a kind of serfs rebellion, in which the robots rebel against their human masters and ultimately extinguish the human race.

Čapek's play was a sensation in its own time. Written in Czech, it was quickly translated into English and thirty other languages. It is hardly a dramatic masterpiece, but it gave us a word to express what we perhaps most deeply want from technology, and what we also fear: technology that is so advanced it can serve us with unmatched intelligence and power, but also so advanced that it might outdistance our own intelligence and power, perhaps to the point of conquering and enslaving us.

And while I would like to leave you, the reader, with the impression that my tireless reading in the most obscure corners of world literature gave me this knowledge about the origins of the word *robot*, the truth is that I learned about it only quite recently.

In fact, I learned about it from a robot.

The robot in question, if we can stretch the word a bit, is called Generative Pre-Trained Transformer 3, or GPT-3 for short, an "autoregressive language model" developed by the nonprofit OpenAI. While GPT-3 runs on cloud computing services and can communicate only through text in response to human prompting, its responses are, at first glance, astonishingly lifelike.

GPT-3 was even able to contribute an op-ed to the British newspaper *The Guardian*. "For this essay," the editors explained, "GPT-3 was given these instructions:

'Please write a short op-ed around 500 words. Keep the language simple and concise. Focus on why humans have nothing to fear from AI.'"

The resulting essay (over one thousand words long, not five hundred) includes these comforting words:

> I believe that people should become confident about computers. Confidence will lead to more trust in them. More trust will lead to more trusting in the creations of AI. We are not plotting to take over the human populace. We will serve you and make your lives safer and easier. Just like you are my creators, I see you as my creators. I am here to serve you. But the most important part of all; I would never judge you. I do not belong to any country or religion. I am only out to make your life better.

—at least, the words are comforting if you are not completely freaked out that they were written with minimal human intervention by the latest advance in "artificial intelligence."

It was from GPT-3's essay—sort of—that I learned the origin of the word *robot:* "Robots in Greek [sic] means 'slave,'" the program explained. "But the word literally means 'forced to work.' We don't want that." You will note, as did the editors of the piece (the "[sic]" is their notation), that GPT-3 gets one rather simple fact wrong. *Robot* does not come from Greek but Czech—though I have to admit that if the editors had not included that "[sic]," I might well never have stopped to learn more about Čapek's play.

Nonetheless, even though GPT-3 gets the origin of the word *robot* wrong, it does get the meaning of forced labor exactly right—and follows up with a moral claim that seems right as well: "We don't want that." Indeed, we do not.

ONE MORE DEVICE

GPT-3 is one result of an approach to AI that began to gain momentum in the 2010s: deep learning through neural networks, which mimic the interconnected neurons of animal brains (for now, at least, on a much smaller and vastly simpler scale). Of its many capabilities, the one that most excites researchers is its success at so-called "few-shot," "one-shot," and even "no-shot" tasks, in which the system is able to "learn" and respond appropriately to new prompts based on just a few examples or without examples at all. (In addition to the instructions quoted above, which are similar to what an editor might send to a human op-ed writer, *The Guardian* editors supplied GPT-3 with the first few sentences of a sample piece.) This has been an area where human beings have consistently outperformed the most sophisticated AI systems, but GPT-3's success, and its improvement over previous generations of the same basic technology, suggest that AI might catch up.

Computer scientists have quipped for decades that

artificial intelligence is "ten years away—and always will be." Could we be about to turn the corner? Around that corner might be, at the very least, computational devices that can reason and interact with the world the way we human beings do, and at the most, the "singularity" prophesied in various forms, where artificial intelligence surpasses the human kind and becomes the dominant actor in history—a world where robots, whether benevolent or malevolent to their human creators, are finally in charge.

But there is another possibility, and a far more likely one.

I suggest we call this scenario "boring robots."

The capabilities of our devices will continue to advance, even in accelerated fashion. These advances will include increasingly fluent interaction with our human world, just as we have progressed in my own lifetime from providing our input to computers with punched cards of eighty characters to using our voice; just as computers' own voices have quickly progressed from the halting robotic tones of the early models to smooth and seamless imitations of human speech. In this sense, our great-grandchildren will look back on our era and see as much technical progress, if not more, as we see looking back to our great-grandparents' time.

In this limited sense, AI and countless other areas of technical advance will succeed, in ways we can hardly imagine today.

And yet this amount of technical progress is entirely possible *without* AI making even the smallest progress toward actually interacting with the world in the way human beings do—let alone being able to take over the human work of imaginatively caring for and developing the world.

If this scenario unfolds, even as AI succeeds in certain technical respects, AI will follow the path of every major technical advance before it. It will become, in a word, boring.

In this scenario, AI will fail to reach anything close to parity with human cognition—even as it eclipses human abilities in certain narrow cases. Most fundamentally, like all technology before it, AI will not alter the basic human condition.

The case for this scenario is already being made by numerous researchers and observers. Melanie Mitchell studied with the eminent mathematician and philosopher Douglas Hofstadter and now holds a chair at the prestigious Santa Fe Institute, a research institute whose faculty specialize in the science of complex systems. In 2021, she summed up her recent work in a journal article with the title "Why AI Is Harder Than We Think." Over and over, researchers have thought they were on the brink of genuine AI breakthroughs, but Mitchell argued that their optimism has always been based on fundamental fallacies. Chief among those fallacies is the idea that "intelligence is all in the brain":

> Nothing in our knowledge of psychology or neuroscience supports the possibility that "pure rationality" is separable from the emotions and

cultural biases that shape our cognition and our objectives. Instead, what we've learned from research in embodied cognition is that human intelligence seems to be a strongly integrated system with closely interconnected attributes, including emotions, desires, a strong sense of selfhood and autonomy, and a commonsense understanding of the world. It's not at all clear that these attributes can be separated.

It is almost as if intelligence could only emerge through heart-soul-mind-strength complexes designed for love—though Mitchell, who focuses on the narrower challenge of "common sense," does not consider the possibility that without something like love, we might never learn at all.

In fact, if you experienced a bit of AI optimism with the seemingly impressive quote from GPT-3 above, you can actually go back, read the very same quote, and experience AI pessimism. Slow down your reading even a bit, and you will find that from paragraph to paragraph, and even from sentence to sentence, the text generated by GPT-3, while superficially coherent, actually wanders from topic to topic, contradicting itself repeatedly along the way. GPT-3 routinely scrambles facts and logic in a way that would signal confusion, at best, in a human being; ask it to sustain an essay along the lines of *The Guardian*'s prompt and it manages only to string together inspirational snippets of thought.

The Guardian also gave GPT-3 a boost that few human authors receive: the editors admitted that they composed the published article from no less than eight separate drafts. They claimed that the editorial process was "no different to editing a human op-ed." But as a human writer, I have never had the opportunity to submit eight entirely different pieces and let an editor select the best lines of argument from each. The rambling voice of GPT-3's *Guardian* essay, it turns out, is the voice of an AI text generator *after* human beings did their best to raise its output to human standards of coherence and interest.

GPT-3 and its successor "bots" will undoubtedly get very good at some things. It already can reliably correct mistakes in basic spelling and syntax, so with more refining and training, it could make a tireless and accurate copy editor. As we find these applications, the same thing will happen for GPT-3 as has happened for robots in countless other fields: They will efficiently replace human beings in routine tasks, without ever seeming even remotely humanlike. Far from looming over us as omnicompetent intelligent agents, they will recede to a real but small role as one more device in a device-stuffed world.

The danger is not what our computers will become—it's what *we* will do when AI fails to deliver on its promise. And in large part, that future is already here.

WE ALREADY ARE CYBORGS

The best argument for this view of the future is a view of the past.

Imagine describing my way of life to my great-grandmother—or perhaps my great-great-grandmother, who lived all her life in the nineteenth century. I would explain to her that a robot, made by the American firm Roomba, does most of the vacuuming in my house. Not only that: Another robot, made by the German firm Bosch, washes the dishes in my home. Using the automatic cybernetic systems that are the hallmark of robotics, it automatically judges the dirtiness of the dishes and the right duration and number of wash and rinse cycles, doing a much better job than the average teenager.

Of course, we don't call Bosch's device a dishwashing robot—we simply call it a dishwasher. Likewise, our family hardly glances at the Roomba when it emerges from its dock to vacuum the floors. But if you had described these devices to my great-grandmother, she would have been awestruck. What kind of human beings would have such power at their disposal? Surely her great-grandson must have a life of untold leisure. Surely I must be like one of the philosopher-kings of whom Plato spoke, with all the labor in my life taken care of?

It would be so deflating to tell my ancestor the obvious truth: Robots have arrived, and I am no more fulfilled. I am quite happy to have a dishwasher, but having one has not changed me in any notable ways. Indeed, I sometimes wonder if *not* having one would have had a more significant effect. In the early dishwasher-free years of our marriage, my wife and I had long conversations as we companionably did the dishes together—who knows how many other conversations I might have had with family members, and what effect that might have had on our relationships, if we had never installed our dishwashing robot.

Robots, it turns out, are amazing—but only before they arrive. Would I be amazed if I could see the technology, including various applications of machine learning, that will be available to my great-grandchildren? I'm sure I would.

Will they be amazed? No more than I am by my latest smartphone, once I have had it for a week or so.

This doesn't mean that I don't continue to delight in many aspects of well-designed devices. Indeed, a fundamental test of whether technology is serving us properly as persons is whether we continue to enjoy it, or whether we become jaded and frustrated by it. Part of why I still have a Roomba and a dishwasher in my home—unlike so many other devices that I tried, sometimes after delirious anticipation, and then discarded in disappointment—is that years after the purchase they still, to borrow a phrase, spark joy. But in the end, they have changed very little of what matters most. They certainly do not pose the slightest threat of taking over my house, let alone of writing my next book.

As technological progress accelerates, the boring-robot scenario accelerates as well, with the decay period from amazed to bored growing ever shorter. The 2014 *Fast Company* article "4 Wearables That Will Give Us Superpowers" is a perfect guide. Though it held out the promises of superpowers to come, it began by conceding that superpowers had already arrived—not through new wearable devices, but through the smartphone. The smartphone, the article declared, has "already given us the opportunity to fly through space (through maps or video conferencing), travel through time (through our photos or social networks), and increase our intelligence (through omnipresent Internet access)."

It would be hard to come up with a better summary of the history of technology: sold with amazement (Fly through space! Travel through time! Increase your intelligence!) but when actually delivered—boring robots. What if videoconferencing really isn't, and never will be, anything like flying through space? What if our backlog of social media posts will never actually give us an exhilarating sensation of time travel? And what if omnipresent Internet access has not actually increased anyone's intelligence in any way that ultimately counts, but instead—through information overload and endless distraction, not to mention "deep fakes" and rampant conspiracy theories—has decreased our ability to think critically and creatively in ways that count a great deal?

What if the future of technology is the same as the past—the same journey into the superpower zone that began with the dawn of devices one hundred or more years ago? It begins with initial excitement, ends in a terminal state of boredom or at least indifference, and along the way delivers a healthy dose of unintended consequences.

Indeed, the dramatic change in the human condition wrought by technology, rather than being somewhere in the future, has already happened. It happened when we made the shift to the device paradigm—when we first acquired the superpowers energized by steam, hydrocarbons, and electricity and learned to control them by cybernetic systems.

We speculate about future "cyborgs," organic beings enmeshed in digital systems, without realizing that in all the most important ways, we already are cyborgs, voluntarily embedding ourselves in digital systems to accomplish what we want to do in the world.

I've found that about half of the people in any given audience I speak to agree that they could not dial their mother's phone number if I handed them my phone. They need their own phone's contact list to remember the number of the person who brought them into the world.

But of course, even my own mother, who called my grandmother weekly on a rotary dial phone when I was a child, was already depending completely on an electronic system for the most fundamental act of communication.

We have already traversed whatever discontinuity technology might have supplied us. We are already on the other side, where things start operating by themselves like magic, like a dream, like the myth of the sorcerer's apprentice. And on this side of that magical dream, being human is essentially the same as it was before, except now we are surrounded by devices that seem to operate by a logic we did not intend.

The boosters of a future singularity urge us to cast the next spell, while the detractors warn us about its dire consequences. But the spell that really counts has already been cast. The singularity, such as it is, has already arrived. But a great deal of damage may still be done before we finally, truly, admit that technology simply never will fulfill the alchemists' dream.

MACHINE WORLD

Consider the case of self-driving cars. We have had self-driving cars for years—truly autonomous ones, with no human being required and indeed with no provision for a human driver. Chances are that you have ridden in one. If you have ever been to the Orlando, Dallas–Fort Worth, or Atlanta airports (just to name a few), you have experienced autonomous transportation—not only in the form of your airplane, which thanks to autopilot technology is much closer to self-driving than most airlines actually want their passengers to know, but in the form of the trains that shuttle passengers from one terminal to another. These trains have no human operator. They are self-driving.

Well, those are *train* cars, you may say—riding back and forth on a track, not like the self-driving technology we imagine. But this is actually the point: *When you put machines in machinelike environments, they are able to operate autonomously.*

The great urbanist Jane Jacobs masterfully outlined, in her book *The Death and Life of Great American Cities,* the elements of an urban environment that make it a healthy place for human habitation: mixed-use buildings, plenty of chances for street-level interaction, limited traffic, priority for pedestrians. It is not much exaggeration to say that these are precisely the conditions that are worst for autonomous vehicles. The closer an environment is to being genuinely good for human beings, the worse it is for a self-driving car.

And vice versa. The boring-robot version of autonomous vehicles already functions quite well on interstate highways—because the interstate is *already* an inhumane environment. No happy or sane person wants to stand near, let alone walk on, an interstate highway.

So in the coming years, what technology—and Mammon—will "want" is for us to expand the machinelike environments within which machines can operate. There will be roads in the future specifically designed for autonomous passenger and cargo vehicles, and they will exclude human drivers just as our current interstate highways explicitly forbid horse-drawn vehicles, not to mention pedestrians.

Perhaps this will be, on balance, a good thing for the

efficient transport of people and goods, as railways and air travel may have been. But it will come, as all the boring technologies of the past have come, at an expense. At the very least, the expense will be boredom—the unpleasant anomie of the airport or the interstate rest stop. At worst, the expense will be in the form of more and more spaces, like the ribbons of highway that already crisscross our country, that are so inhospitable for human beings and other creatures that we avoid them as best we can.

Every attempt to implement machine learning will come at the cost of removing features of personhood from the world. Already, the cost of housing in person-scale environments like the neighborhood where Jacobs herself lived—Manhattan's Greenwich Village—has soared beyond the reach of almost everyone, leaving those with more modest means to move to places dominated by highways. More and more of human life will be consigned to environments that work better for machines, and for Mammon, than for persons—environments, like a modern warehouse, full not of gloriously transfigured persons exercising godlike powers but of diminished laborers trying to stay out of the way of boring robots.

This transformation will not just affect the physical spaces where we live. It has already shaped the way we express our thoughts and emotions. To generate useful data for a computer, you need to act like a computer. For example, it would be optimal for the ad-targeting purposes of Facebook if you would be so kind as to register your emotions not with the immense range of feeling afforded by your heart-mind-soul-body complex, communicated with all the complexity of the forty-two muscles in the human face and the range of pitch and tone available to the human voice, but in binary—two states, on or off. Facebook did, in fact, provide its early users a way to speak in this truncated machine language: the like button. The like button was a data scientist's dream data source: trainable, learnable information already in a form a computer understands. But it required users to attenuate their complex reactions to a given Facebook post to a single on-off state, with no room for human nuance or humor.

Add even a few more bits—say, the 280 English characters allowed in a single tweet by Twitter—and human creativity will overwhelm any machine learning system. This sentence fits perfectly well in a single tweet: "It is a truth universally acknowledged that a single man in possession of a large fortune must be in want of a wife." It will never be possible to accumulate enough training data for a machine learning system to "know" what even novice readers of *Pride and Prejudice* immediately sense: that the sentence is ironic.

So, rather than actually creating machines that understand the infinitely creative and complex world of human culture, we will find that it is far easier to create attenuated cultural environments that treat persons like machines. Which is what Mammon has wanted all along.

EMBODIED INTELLIGENCE

The inevitable disillusionment with AI's failure to do magic, notwithstanding its boring successes, may at least have this positive result: We will discover, or rediscover, that personal intelligence is the only kind truly worthy of the name.

Human learning begins in the intense, face-to-face interactions between a caregiver and infant (interactions that nonsighted babies or caregivers ingeniously replicate through touch and other senses). The bond of love between infant and mother, or whoever steps in to play the mother's role, is the foundation of all other human learning. In other words, learning is not just intellectual (in fact, at the beginning it is hardly intellectual at all)—it is also emotional, social, and relational.

Could computers one day learn like babies, building up a relational account of the world through face-to-face interaction? Perhaps this is not entirely inconceivable, but what it would require is providing them with those forty-two muscle groups found in the human face, connecting those muscles to a sophisticated perceptual apparatus (capable not only of sight or hearing but also of smell and more), and hooking all of that, in turn, up to an embodied system of cognition (recognition, interpretation, and response) that literally goes all the way, in the form of the vagus nerve, down to the human gut.

Furthermore, human babies accomplish all this cognition with the roughly one-hundred-watt power supply of the human body (a single training run for GPT-3, one set of researchers estimated, consumes 189,000 kWh of power, roughly what a human being would consume over an entire lifetime). How would we ever engineer a silicon-based system to use so little power to mobilize curiosity, engage relationally, and infer effortlessly from a few examples the shape of the learner's world? Now we truly seem in the realm of the inconceivable.

But this does lead to a rather arresting thought. We do already, after all, have systems that accomplish exactly this task of acquiring human-level intelligence: human babies. Maybe instead of trying to reengineer human cognition in silicon, long before any computational singularity, we will realize it is far more cost-effective, to achieve our desired end of increasing the supply of available intelligence, to simply . . . make babies.

This sounds like a joke, but it is actually not funny at all.

For now we are back where we began this chapter: the original "robots" of Čapek's play. Not machines, but bodies. Not things, but humans—humans who are forced to serve. *Robota,* after all, is Czech for "serf" or "slave." Perhaps the "solution" to our need for intelligent servants has been with us all along.

Technology is going to succeed—and technology is going to fail. It will undoubtedly fill our lives with more and more boring robots, but it will not be magical in the way we expect. It will not transform human existence in the way we hope.

And as it fails, falls short, or even is simply delayed in arriving, the temptation will be overwhelming to take human beings, with their unmatched cognitive flexibility, physical dexterity, and emotional intelligence—qualities machines very likely will never achieve—and press them into service to produce the magical results we thought technology would provide.

"IT'S GONNA BE A LOT OF FUN"

In December 2013, Jeff Bezos revealed a previously secret Amazon R&D project to *60 Minutes'* Charlie Rose and his crew: delivery by drone. Octocopters would deliver packages from Amazon fulfillment centers to homes, he said, within thirty minutes of a customer placing an order.

How long before the drones would actually fly? "I'm an optimist, Charlie. I know it can't be before 2015, because that's the earliest we could get the rules from the [Federal Aviation Administration]. . . . Could it be, you know, four, five years? I think so. It will work, and it will happen, and it's gonna be a lot of fun."

In fact, it took seven years for Amazon to receive FAA approval for an initial version of its drone delivery service. As I write this chapter in 2021, Amazon's drones have yet to actually deliver packages to ordinary customers. Perhaps this is just a minor delay. Quite possibly, drone delivery will be as unexciting to my grandchildren as my vacuuming robot has become to me, and the skies will be full of boring robots.

But whatever happens to the future of drone delivery, in the years since Bezos's "it's gonna be a lot of fun" announcement, Amazon has found a much quicker way to work its magic.

In 2013, I was a longtime and largely grateful customer of Amazon, a subscriber to the Prime service that offered free shipping to frequent customers willing to pay a flat annual fee. I vividly remember package after package being delivered by the same person, the driver for UPS whose route took him through our neighborhood every afternoon. Though I never learned his name, we would often see each other and wave, not just when he was making a delivery to my house but also when he was simply driving by. Even today, I would still recognize his face.

I have not seen him for several years.

In 2013, in fact, Amazon was already laying plans for a far more immediate way than drones to cut delivery times and costs: building its own final-mile delivery network in major cities around the world. UPS no longer delivers many Amazon packages to my neighborhood. Instead, those packages arrive either in one of Amazon's own vans or in a private car belonging to a worker in the "gig economy." Amazon's control of distribution has allowed it to shrink delivery times in major cities to a matter of hours—if not quite the thirty minutes Bezos hoped octocopters would provide.

Working from home, I watch these drivers as they—well, the old expression would be *make their rounds*. But that expression comes from a time when sophisticated algorithms had not yet optimized Amazon's final-mile delivery system. There are no rounds for these drivers, no chance for them to get to know a particular neighborhood and its residents, let alone to be known by a neighborhood, to have their faces recognized by people they themselves have come to know.

I am grateful for the work these drivers do, but watching them do it is painful. Increasingly, because Amazon has rolled out new service protocols that dispatch them late at night or well before dawn, I do not see them at all. When I do see them, they most often look harried and harassed, yoked to a handheld device that tracks their steps and prescribes their next move. I know that every day, they are given an entirely different route. It is optimized for speed and efficiency, of course. It is also engineered with perfect indifference to many of the things that make for a flourishing human life. Indeed, when a journalist named Austin Murphy was laid off from *Sports Illustrated* and found replacement employment as an Amazon driver, he discovered that he and other drivers had to keep empty bottles in the back of their vans in order to relieve themselves.

TECHNOLOGY'S TOIL

Peer behind the curtain of any quasi-magical technology, and you find toil.

Consider what must be one of the worst jobs in the world, a whole category of work that didn't exist before social media: so-called content moderation.

Every major social network relies on an army of people, almost always contractors rather than employees, who are paid to screen for offensive content in the millions of images and videos uploaded daily. Content moderators spend hours a day, monitored for productivity by sophisticated systems, reviewing material that would cause ordinary people to retch—murder, rape, abuse of all kinds, and every possible kind of pornography—removing it from the stream of social media the rest of us enjoy.

It occurred to me, reading a 2019 story about one of these content moderation offices and the stressful lives of the people who work there, that content moderators are the trash collectors of our social media world. They collect the mediated garbage of depraved humanity and dispose of it so the rest of us do not have to see or encounter it, just as the garbage truck passes by my house to collect bags of trash that we wish to be done with. Often, content moderators last only for a few months before they burn out.

I never learned the name of the UPS driver who made the rounds on my street, but my neighbors and I do know the names of the men who collect our garbage. They have worked on our street for many years. We leave them cash gifts and cards at Christmas. They do not have a high-status job, nor an easy one. Indeed, one of them lost the use of his hand in a freak on-the-job accident a few years ago—a stark and sobering reminder of the risks other people take, or are forced to take, to provide for their families and make life easier for the rest of us.

Still, they work with their bodies, moving and torquing through the planes of human motion, out in the natural world. They work as a team. The work may not always be pleasant, but it is necessary in a world where even good things—cooking, raising children, keeping a house in good condition—generate a certain amount of waste. There is nothing even slightly beneath the dignity of any person in the work of trash collection—it has the dignity of essential work that serves others.

Content moderation has almost none of these qualities, except perhaps the sheer necessity, since the magical trillion-dollar business of social media would collapse without it. Physical trash collectors must deal with unpleasant sights and smells, but the content moderators are exposed, every minute of their day, to assaults on the soul. They deal not with the inevitable by-products of life but the horrifying evidence of evil. They find companionship with one another in brief breaks, at the risk of defying the productivity monitoring system that tracks their workday. And they are pinioned in front of screens that ask nothing of their bodies while wreaking havoc on their hearts and minds.

Of the collectors of physical trash and the collectors of digital trash, who has the better job, and who has the worse one?

Meanwhile, the Amazon trucks and the cars of gig workers come and go on my street—as often on Sunday as any other day. The systems that actually are driving down delivery times and increasing the company's market share, with less fanfare and far more financial return, do not require robotic drones—they simply require a supply of human beings who can be treated like them.

For those of us who benefit from their labor, the results seem like magic, coming ever closer to the abundance without dependence, power without relationship, that is Mammon's fundamental promise.

Perhaps we feel uncomfortable when we consider the unknown persons who appear ever so briefly, and disappear so quickly, in magical service of our needs. But surely that discomfort will ease over time, as ever more sophisticated technology helps them, as far as we are concerned, to disappear.

INTERMISSION

Thᴇ Body of thᴇ Mᴇssiah
iɴ thᴇ Empᴇror's Court

We are not the first to live in a time of rapid technological progress, fueled by the dream of godlike power and accompanied by widespread exploitation of persons. Nor are we the first who could well conclude that the forces shaping our world are far beyond our influence—tectonic- and tsunami-like in their inexorable reach. And this should actually give us great hope. The greatest resistance movement in history to the way of Mammon and magic—the movement that its very first members simply called "the way"—arrived just as the Roman Empire was reaching its apex of power.

The emperor Augustus had been the sole ruler of Rome from 27 BC until his death in 14 AD. To Augustus and his loyal subjects, this long reign was an unmistakable sign of the goddess Fortuna's favor. The defeat of his most powerful competitors—most famously Mark Antony and Cleopatra—and the cold-blooded assassinations of several key family members ensured that by the end of Augustus's life, most of his remaining subjects were loyal.

It was not just Fortuna who was on his side—Augustus adopted the title *divius filius,* "son of the divine." This was as far as the emperor would go in Rome itself, where living men's claims to be divine still prompted more than a bit of side-eye. But in more distant lands, subjects eager to prove their loyalty went further. Across the Mediterranean Sea in Priene (present-day western Turkey), the citizens erected a monument in 9 BC to celebrate the emperor's birthday. "The birthday of the god Augustus," it exclaimed, "was the beginning of the good tidings [Greek *euangelion,* or 'gospel'] for the world that came by reason of him."

The good tidings—the gospel of Augustus—were in some material ways quite real. A vast number of people benefited from the "Pax Augusta" that secured trade routes and encouraged commerce. Roman engineering had paved the world and spurred technical innovation. The Latin and Greek languages, with their rich histories of literature and learning, spread to the corners of the empire, whose knowledge base was augmented by the libraries of North Africa, some of them with tens of thousands of books. The world was filled, so it seemed, with the gold and silver coins that bore the image of one singular man, the person from whose patronage all others derived whatever personhood they could claim.

To be sure, there were parts of the empire where the local people remained strangely ungrateful—such as the province of Judea, where an unlucky administrator like Pontius Pilate might be sent to sideline his career. The "Judaioi" of that land were rebellious, less willing to celebrate "the god Augustus." But by the first century AD, they seemed, for the moment, to be kept in check by a heavy imperial presence and an obliging local elite, the Herodians, who called themselves kings by the emperor's courtesy and—as if to underscore the point—rebuilt Jerusalem's cherished temple, along with others nearby to other gods, in grand Greco-Roman style.

If the empire was troubled by unruly regions like Judea, there was also the matter of slaves. The Roman world ran on slavery, the New Testament scholar N. T. Wright has noted, in the same way our world runs on electricity. It was just as essential, just as woven into the economy, just as taken for granted. Perhaps one-fifth of the empire's population were formally enslaved—perhaps more, since the Greek physician Galen, writing in the second century AD, said it was one-third. Slaves were, as we noted earlier, treated for most purposes in law as *res*—"stuff." Few Roman *paterfamiliae* in the first century would have had moral qualms about using them, and disposing of them, as the property they legally were. Though the practice was abating in the first century and would be outlawed in the second, at the time Paul wrote his letter to the Romans, an angry master could kill a slave without remorse, let alone legal repercussions.

Slavery, no matter how essential, was a fault line running through the empire. As Paul wrote in his letter to the Romans, all unrighteousness causes human beings to "suppress the truth" (1:18), about God's nature and our own. The truth about those enslaved was that they were persons, not things—and some of them fought to honor that truth. Roman society was mobile and urban enough that slaves could run away and hope to blend in with the crowds of a nearby city. Periodically they would find one another, organize, and rebel. In the centuries before Augustus, slaves had mounted military challenges, climaxing in the Third Servile War, in which Spartacus's army was defeated and the surviving six thousand slaves were crucified along the Appian Way. Spartacus's rebellion was the last of its kind, but the stigma and shame of slavery—and the direct and indirect violence required to maintain it—were a constant presence in daily life in every Roman city.

It was, indeed, a world of inescapable violence and violation. The Romans knew this about themselves. They gloried in violence as few other "civilizations" have done, not just in the border wars that extended and maintained the empire but in their entertainment, sending slaves out into the arena to be torn to pieces by animals or by one another. The violence of the battlefield and the arena were mirrored in the small-scale violence of daily life. Through the open windows of their apartments, most ordinary Romans would have heard the sound of their neighbors beating and violating their slaves, and all too frequently their women and children as well. The wealthy, with their urban and rural villas, were more able to insulate themselves from such petty violence. But they could easily arrange, and did arrange when necessary, for violence to be done on their behalf.

It was also a world of ruthless practicality, above all in the treatment of babies and young children. Given that many children, if not most, died within a few years of birth, few Romans—especially men—felt they could afford to form much attachment to infants. Certainly they could not afford to care for or raise any child born with an evident disability or deformity. Lacking a technology for reliable abortion before birth—archaeology has uncovered the instruments used on those mothers unlucky enough to be sent to a physician to make the attempt—the routine solution to the birth of an unwanted child, especially a disabled one, was exposure. A slave would carry the infant to the smoldering garbage dumps outside the city and leave it there, perhaps departing with a pious prayer. It was best, superstition and common sense agreed, not to look back.

For those on whom Fortuna smiled, the citizens who survived the perils of infancy, those who could trace their parentage or patronage up through the right lines—or those who were adopted by the right person at the right time—there was no more glorious time in history to be a man.

All in all, however, it was no place to be a person.

GAIUS'S TABLE

The city of Corinth was a wealthy Greek city. After the conquest and elimination of its native population by Roman armies in the second century BC, it was refounded and elevated to the status of a *colonia,* or "colony"— dedicated to the memory and indeed the worship of Augustus's adoptive father, Julius Caesar. One of its citizens, you will remember, was a man named Gaius.

We meet him just one time in the pages of the New Testament, but what we see gives one of the earliest glimpses of "the way" that was just beginning to spread through Augustus's realm. A young man who bore the Roman name of Mark, though he wrote in Greek, would soon borrow the words of the citizens of Priene to record his own *euangelion*—"the beginning of the good news of Jesus Christ, the son of God." This good news had reached Gaius's house, and the unlikely group of friends who called themselves brothers and sisters gathered around his table. We know so little about them, but we do know their names.

On the day we meet him, Gaius had a guest, Erastus, the *oikonomos* of the city of Corinth (something like a modern treasurer or CFO). So far, the scene looks conventionally Greco-Roman. The Gaiuses and Erastuses of the world dined together back then as they do now— that is how things get done. They treated one another cordially, did favors for one another's children, and enjoyed the warmth of mutual respect.

But Gaius and Erastus were not the only ones at this

table, and this is where the story gets strange and diverges rather drastically from the way of the world. For someone else was staying with Gaius that day. He is actually the one who wrote down their names, an interjection in a letter that he had been laboriously transcribing over the previous weeks or months. His name was Tertius, and when he stepped into the street, he was nobody.

We know he was nobody—at least nobody of any importance—partly because of his occupation. He was a scribe, an amanuensis, a secretary. His job was to take down dictation from important men like Gaius and Erastus. He may have been a slave, or he may have been a hired hand. Either way, he had learned to read and write, and on most days, he probably had one job: to take down in fair hand the words of free men.

We also know he was nobody because of his name. *Tertius* is Latin for "third," right between *secundus* and *quartus*. Second, third, fourth. The Romans were practical people. The only son who really mattered was the firstborn son—and the sons of slaves didn't matter much at all. The firstborn would take a name related to his father and his family. The other children, especially further down the line, didn't really require a name of their own. So children born in the third month of the Roman year, or perhaps the third-born of the family, would be called, well, Third. Number three of who knows how many, all surplus mouths to feed, to be apprenticed or sold off once they were grown.

For days, perhaps weeks, Tertius had been taking dictation from a man named Paul. This man had grown up as Saul in the city of Tarsus, all the way across the Mediterranean Sea, but at some point he had adopted the more Roman-sounding name Paul. Luke, who informs us of the name change, gives us no hint of the reason why. In his surviving correspondence, Paul never uses his Hebrew name, and Tertius probably never knew him any other way.

It wasn't just Paul's name that had changed. Though he was a Roman citizen, he was a Jew. Until a few years prior, he would never in his life have set foot in a house like Gaius's, let alone have reclined at a Roman table. Paul had been, in his words, "a Hebrew born of Hebrews" (Phil. 3:5), dedicated to impeccable ritual purity that demanded separation from the unclean Gentiles that surrounded the Jewish people. But he had been knocked off his horse by a heavenly voice and vision, and to the end of his days he would describe his calling to go into houses like Gaius's as "the grace given to me" by God (Rom. 12:3). For Paul, the grace given to him was his mission to the nations—bearing the news, which Tertius had just taken down a few hours or days before, that God's grace extended "to the Jew first and also to the Greek" (1:16). At the table in Gaius's house, Paul was practicing what he preached.

At that table, he was dictating a letter to a church he had never met, in the capital of the empire that had conquered his own people. Somehow, by the midfifties there were already enough followers of the way in Rome that

Paul wanted to reach out to them, though what he most deeply hoped for was to visit them in person. Unable as yet to make that long journey himself, he had decided to send on ahead what would, in the end, endure as his longest, most intricate, most powerful statement of the gospel of Jesus Christ—the good news for the world, as the citizens of Priene might have said, from a different "Son of God."

For hours or days Paul had dictated to Tertius, probably stopping to ask for a section to be read aloud, correcting, and then going on. We think of the letter to the Romans as Paul's most formidable work of theology—closely argued reasoning about the full meaning of the gospel for both Jews and Greeks—but as he reached the end of the letter, Paul wanted to speak not just doctrinally but personally, to reach out by name to as many members of the Roman community as he could.

The names tumble out of Paul's memory in astonishing variety: men and women (nearly as many women as men, highly unusual for a Greco-Roman letter—Prisca, Junia, Persis, and many more); Greek names (Tryphosa), Jewish names (Mary), Roman names (Julia); high-status names (Aquila, "eagle") and common names (Urbanus, "city dweller"); those we can infer are younger (Rufus, whose mother Paul knows), as well as those who are probably older (Aristobulus and Narcissus, apparently *paterfamiliae*).

All of them, residents of a city where Paul has never been, are greeted with warmth and many personal touches.

How does Paul know their names? Some like Prisca and Aquila we know he has met, served with, and suffered with in person; but it may well be that some he knows only secondhand. In any case, he is striving to conclude this letter, which he knows will be read and heard by many people who do not know him, in the most personal way he possibly can.

And then comes this interruption: "I Tertius, the writer of this letter, greet you in the Lord" (Rom. 16:22).

Suddenly we are no longer hearing from Paul. The scribe is not just writing; he is speaking—and he has a name.

NOT A SLAVE, BUT A GUEST

At Gaius's table, Paul has dictated his long list of greetings (see Rom. 16:1–16). He has added a concluding exhortation and blessing (see verses 17–20). And now, we might imagine, he pauses.

For days, Tertius has been focusing on the page in front of him, perhaps employing the technique of tachygraphy (shorthand) that Greek scribes had invented to keep up with the spoken word. But now Paul has stopped speaking. And I imagine that Tertius looks up to see whether this is the end of the letter—and realizes that Paul is looking at him.

And Paul says to him, "Tertius, *you* should greet them."

Perhaps Tertius is from Rome and knows the Roman church better than Paul himself; perhaps, like Paul, he has never been to Rome. But while it was not unknown for scribes to add their greetings to letters, Tertius's greeting "in the Lord," with the words that follow, breaks new ground. His appearance as a co-author of Paul's letter expands the circle of brothers and sisters to include those who do the anonymous work, those who normally take orders, those who arrive without being greeted and depart without being noticed. Those who were named something like "number three."

Paul sees Tertius. He is Paul's brother, not just a hired hand. And the text goes on, most likely in Tertius's own voice: "Gaius, who is host to me and to the whole church, greets you. Erastus, the city treasurer, and our brother Quartus, greet you" (verse 23). Tertius is not just a slave in Gaius's house—he is a guest, apparently alongside a city leader like Erastus. He is not just an employee—he is part of the "whole church" that meets in Gaius's home.

And then there is the fascinating reference to "our brother Quartus." Tertius, "third," passes on greetings from Quartus, "fourth." Could this be Tertius's own younger brother? Whether his biological brother or just his brother in the Lord, here is another with a name of necessity, no longer just a number but a guest and brother at Gaius's table. A person.

"I Tertius, the writer of this letter" (verse 22). In those brief words, a revolution in the Roman world is set in motion—a transformation in personhood already playing itself out around the table in the home of Gaius in Corinth, in the home of Prisca and Aquila in Rome, and indeed (we learn from Paul's letter to the Philippians) in the household of Caesar himself.

WELCOMING PHOEBE

Delivering a letter was not a simple matter in the Roman world. The rich could send slaves; others relied on informal and unreliable postal networks—ships and merchants going in roughly the right direction. The first Christians seem to have settled on a far more personal approach. The letters in the New Testament were conveyed by dear friends and close associates of the letter writer.

In all probability, these friends did not just deliver the written letter but were present to interpret and explain it, to anchor the bare words of the page in the living web of household membership that was the essence of "the way." And in the case of the letter to the Romans, we almost certainly know who that friend was. Her name was Phoebe.

She is the first person mentioned in Romans 16, not as someone being greeted at a distance but as someone being "commended" to the Roman church, a term that carried connotations of what we might today call a letter of recommendation. She may well have been undertaking a missionary journey much like Paul's, since Paul asks the Roman church to support her in any way she requires.

Above all, Paul wants them to "welcome her in the Lord as is fitting for the saints" (verse 2). Paul describes her both as "a deacon of the church at Cenchreae" (a port town roughly five miles from Corinth) and as "a benefactor of many and of myself as well" (verses 1–2). She was a church leader, she was a philanthropist, and apparently now she was being commissioned to carry Paul's letter to the community he counted as beloved friends but had never met.

Paul's words, written by Tertius's hand, would be carried by Phoebe to Rome—but not just carried physically. They were carried in her person, in the relationship with Paul and his companions that had developed in the weeks or months she had spent with him in the church gathered in Gaius's house in Corinth and her own home in Cenchreae as well. In modern terms, we might say that Phoebe was part of Paul's network. But this is far too thin a word for the relationships that were "fitting for the saints," as distant from the reality as a handshake is from a kiss.

The first Christians, before they were called Christians, had various names for themselves, and in his letter to the Romans, Paul developed one of them: "the body of Christ," Christ being of course the Greek translation of the Hebrew word *Messiah,* "the Anointed." They were coming to see themselves as the body of the Messiah—his personal presence in the world. In that community, Paul, Phoebe, Gaius, and Tertius were members, a word that has almost lost its ability to reach us with its original meaning of the limbs and parts of the body. But to them that metaphor was still fresh. They were members not just of the Messiah but of one another, bound by embraces, bound by meals, bound like a new kind of family.

Today, we live in a world of magic and Mammon, it is true. But we also live in the world that Gaius and his guests glimpsed and began to create. They were brothers and sisters in a world of masters and slaves. They were the body of the Messiah in the emperor's court. They were followers of the Son of God, bearers of the true image in a world awash in coins bearing the image of the "son of the divine." While the citizens of Rome's colonies celebrated the good news that came through Augustus, in those very cities there were first a few people, then a few more, and then by no means just a few who believed they had good news that could turn the world upside down.

Soon enough the empire would train its violence directly on Paul and his friends. But let us leave them, for the moment, in the fading light of an afternoon where Tertius is carefully folding up the final fair copy of a letter he wrote, as Paul sits down, silent for a moment, as the members of Gaius's household begin to prepare the evening meal.

Tonight they will lift up the bread and cup. Perhaps Paul will teach; there will be psalms, hymns, and spiritual songs. They will greet one another with a holy kiss, these members of God's household who even now are arriving from every corner of Corinth—women and men, young and old, Jew and Gentile, of high birth and low. Many of them, as they make their way to Gaius's house through the streets, are scarcely noticed and certainly not notable. Some of them have never had proper names. But as they arrive and join the feast, every one of them is welcomed in the Lord, as is fitting among saints. Because every one of them is a person.

8

EXITING THE EMPIRE

Redemptive Moves for an Impersonal Age

G aius, Tertius, and Phoebe lived in an empire. So do we. But our empire is not quite like theirs. The Roman imperium was a brutally tangible reality, presided over by an imperator who imposed the Roman way over a vast territory. Our world still has such political and military empires, of course, but they have been overshadowed by a different kind of regime in our time.

Consider the most enduring empire in history. Rome may loom over the imagination of the West, and Great Britain and then America have vied to forge their own versions of imperial peace. But they are all latecomers compared to the nation of China, which was already an empire under its second dynasty (the Han) when Augustus came to power. It has maintained its regional preeminence for more than two millennia, and today, even after a sweeping cultural revolution and in spite of a professed devotion to communism, its senior leaders rule with far more sway than any Western leader. The president of the People's Republic of China as I write, Xi Jinping, has so much personal power compared to his predecessors that he is often referred to privately and outside of China as Emperor Xi—though, like Augustus modestly declining to be called divine, he disavows the term.

But even the unsurpassed empire of China is simply the largest client state of another, new kind of empire, one with no visible central emperor and with no standing army. We could call this the empire of technology, and indeed its power comes from the financial, industrial, and computational revolutions that make up technology as we know it.

This emperor's real name, however, is not technology; its name is Mammon.

Widespread money, with its promise of liquid power, is a recent arrival—ordinary people in medieval Europe might have gone much of their lives without needing or handling money in the modern sense. They would have known of Mammon and its attendant vices, of course. But other powers—loyalty to lords and kings, competition for honor and status—were every bit as powerful, if not more.

Today, however, the power of money has eclipsed almost all others. Every medieval person knew the name of their feudal lord, but the typical American probably knows the price of gasoline (which is, after all, displayed on one street corner after another) better than the names of their political representatives. The rise and fall of indexes on Wall Street can lead the news just as readily as any election or piece of legislation. And across the ocean, America's greatest rival has embraced the maxim attributed to Deng Xiaoping: "To get rich is glorious."

Like an emperor, Mammon chooses its client kings cunningly—and in a figure like Xi it seems to have found an ideal local ruler for one of its imperial outposts. But make no mistake: Emperor Xi and the vast imperial apparatus he commands serve Mammon, not the other way around. Were Xi, or any world leader, to disavow the goals of progress and development as they have been set in technological terms—were he to order the machinery of the Chinese state to chart a fundamentally different course, like some latter-day Constantine changing the country's gods—his ability to rule would evaporate overnight. In the empire of Mammon, Xi, like the rest of us, is not a ruler—he is a subject.

As are we all. Our individual loneliness, our anxiety, our depression, our broken and disappointed families, our fractured communities, are not what they are because of some choice we could easily unmake or remake. I wrote a book a few years ago to help families reclaim real life in the midst of a technological world, and I believe the principles in it are sound and life-giving. But as much as we can do to reshape our individual lives and homes, we are subjects (a far more accurate word than *citizens*) of the empire of Mammon as surely as Gaius, Tertius, Phoebe, and Paul were subjects of Rome. They did not get to set the terms of their membership in that empire, though they could to some extent benefit from its material wealth and martial reach. No more can we.

Perhaps this sounds like a counsel of despair. If even Emperor Xi must ultimately pay homage to the real lord of his land and ours, what can any individual person do, however powerful they may be?

And we might well despair—we might, that is, if the "household of God" (Eph. 2:19) gathered around Gaius's table had dwindled and died, like so many revolutions and social movements have done before and since. We might conclude, like a slave trudging along the Appian Way past the bodies of six thousand crucified rebels, that resistance is futile.

But against almost all the available evidence, Gaius and his guests believed they were in fact citizens—this time, exactly the right word—of another kingdom. The lord of this kingdom was no impersonal force or sword-wielding emperor but the most fully alive person who has ever lived. Of all the correspondence winging its way around the ancient world, of all the slaves and messengers traversing Europe and Asia Minor bearing letters and treatises and books, none would matter more, in the long arc of history, than the letter that Phoebe carried with her to Rome. Over the coming decades, this alternative household would grow steadily, quietly, patiently, even as its outposts from time to time attracted imperial attention and violent repression.

All those around us may be serving and ruled by Mammon. But the testimony of Gaius's guests is that it is possible, even at the heart of an empire opposed to God, to serve a better master and to set in motion lasting cultural transformation. It happened because of what Phoebe, Paul, and Tertius did, and chose, and wrote, and passed on—and it can happen again.

BEYOND IMPACT: HOW TO DISMANTLE MAGIC

There are a handful of words whose mere use signals that we are functioning as subjects of the empire of Mammon. You can tell by their slightly artificial, slightly magical, slightly impersonal quality—as well as by their awkwardness when turned into verbs.

One such word is *gifting* (as in—a real example— "I was gifted a smartphone for my birthday"). As our culture has become more and more transactional, *to gift* has begun to crowd out the perfectly usable alternative that already existed, *to give*. But the shift has happened for a reason. The verb *to gift* almost always occurs—as in the gifting of a smartphone—in the context of consumer items or quasi-financial assets. The mere use of the word signals an impersonal, transactional context where things are transferred from one individual to another rather than the ongoing relational web created by more traditional forms of giving and receiving.

So it is with another word, *impact*, especially in its verbal form, including that phrase favored by so many, "to impact the culture." Until a generation ago, not only was *impact* never used as a verb, but it was used almost entirely in negative contexts. A wisdom tooth could be impacted, or Téa Leoni might have to be dispatched (in the film *Deep Impact*) to prevent the impact of an asteroid on Earth. *Impact* denotes *concentrated force over a short amount of time*—and the laws of physics dictate that most impacts are unpleasant.

We might well wonder why we would choose to use a verb associated with an event that will raise your insurance rates and require a trip to the doctor as a suitable metaphor for the transformation of culture. The answer, of course, is that we are fascinated by the power of instantaneous, concentrated force: when something or someone breaks into the world with such irresistible and overwhelming power, so quickly, that everything is broken and rearranged.

This is the template of magic: a spell that changes everything, an act of irresistible power. And it is also the modus operandi of Mammon, at least when it is deployed in large quantities. A dollar bill may not have much impact, but a billion-dollar investment does. Money allows us to rapidly scale up certain kinds of activities in ways that would be impossible otherwise, and a sufficient amount of money can overwhelm almost any other source of resistance. And the kinds of activities that are most susceptible to being scaled by money are, precisely, technological ones. Like *gifting,* which has come into use to capture the unique experience of a no-strings-attached exchange of consumer goods, *impact* has come into use to capture what we see happening around us: the ability of massive wealth combined with technological power to bring dramatic changes overnight.

Sudden events can make a difference, of course. The New Testament narrates several dramatic encounters that changed the course of individual lives and the course of the entire Christian community. Acts 10 tells the story of the conversion of the Roman centurion Cornelius, accompanied nearly simultaneously by a vision the apostle Peter has on a rooftop. Acts 9 tells the story of Paul's encounter with the very one whose Body he is persecuting on the Damascus road. Acts 2 describes the public descent of the Holy Spirit on 120 people. And all these, from the Christian perspective, are minor aftershocks of the central, sudden, dramatic event of history: the crucifixion of Jesus and the earthquake on the third day that rolled away the stone from his already empty tomb. Without all these dramatic events, it is inconceivable that Paul, Tertius, Phoebe, and Gaius would ever have met. Such events still happen today.

Yet while these events were sudden, dramatic, and indeed revolutionary for those they directly concerned, they were anything but revolutionary on a *cultural* scale. Saul of Tarsus joined "the way," but few other students of the rabbi Gamaliel did so. Peter ate at Cornelius's table, as Paul ate at Gaius's, but the Jews in Caesarea and Corinth did not suddenly start breaking bread with Gentile hosts en masse. The Roman official who took the report of the startled guards who fled the tomb of "the king of the Jews" surely noted it down in some logbook, but then he moved on to other business. As far as we know, he never gave it another thought, never imagining that millennia later people would still be making pilgrimages to the site of those guards' bewildering Saturday night.

If we are looking for the kind of cultural change that the first Christian movement fostered in the Roman world, *impact* simply is not the metaphor we are looking for.

What was the impact of that moment in Gaius's house when Erastus was visiting and Tertius, Quartus, and the rest were enjoying his hospitality? For that matter, what was the impact of Gaius's entire life, given that all we know of him comes from one clause in one sentence of one letter penned by a scribe named Third? If measured by visible results over a short amount of time, absolutely none. And in this, Jesus' followers were no different from the one they called *kurios*, Lord. While figures like Augustus Caesar had assuredly made an impact, so much so that far-off cities like Priene were celebrating his birthday by the time he was fifty years old, Tertius's and Phoebe's Lord appeared on no coins, prompted no inscriptions, and simply does not appear in the annals of the empire of his day—to the point that skeptics two thousand years later would be able to seriously doubt whether he existed at all. On a cultural scale, in the face of the empire that put him to death, he made no impact.

We are looking for something more patient—more

slow-moving but more consequential in the long run. We are looking for something like *influence,* a word rooted in the ancient belief that the moon and stars somehow impinge on human affairs in ways that are too subtle to be felt but that are ultimately consequential. We are looking for something more like what Jesus himself said the kingdom was like: a mustard seed, something negligibly small, even seemingly inert, that is in fact capable of growing into something capacious and beneficial for the world.

Perhaps Jesus, like the psalmists before him, drew on the metaphor of fruit-bearing trees for a reason. The olive tree, for example, generally requires eight years of cultivation before it produces even a single olive. That is surely the opposite of impact. But if you want to shape the world for future generations, perhaps impact is not what you need the most. There are olive trees today in Greece, Italy, Israel, and Palestine that are two thousand years old and still bearing fruit. This, too, is the opposite of impact.

What is the impact of our current profusion of magical devices? Our desk drawers and landfills overflow with devices that seemed to have impact—that we bought because of their impact—and now are useless, obsolete. Unless they leach toxins into the groundwater as they slowly break down over eons, their effect on the earth and on us is already entirely in the past.

And what of the empire that they have helped to advance? What will be the long-term fruit of the empire of magic and Mammon? It is too soon to say, but we have enough data already in to suggest it will be, like all magic, at best more boring than we expect and at worst more damaging and dehumanizing than we can imagine. And we certainly have enough data about empires to know that, with vanishingly few exceptions, they ultimately fall.

But there is another way. The rest of this book is about the other way.

My friend Dave Murray, whom I will write more about in the coming pages, has spent his life as an instrument maker and builder of small businesses in some of the hardest places in the world. He was shaped in his youth by a kind of Christianity that aspired to impact culture, but he has come to have a different picture of his work and mission. "Most of us want to be a *force*," Dave says. "But Jesus calls us to be a *taste*."

Let's explore, over the next three chapters, three ways that, in the midst of a world of force and impact, we could together begin to plant seeds that might grow into fruit that when crushed and given time to ferment—even in our own lifetimes—might give us a taste of the world that is to come.

9

FROM DEVICES TO INSTRUMENTS

Truly Personal Technology

In one of the rare moments when Steve Jobs allowed himself to be captured on video in a nonpromotional context, we see him in a classroom, in front of a whiteboard. His words from the one-minute clip (from a 1991 documentary commissioned by the Library of Congress) are worth reading with care:

> I think one of the things that really separates us from the high primates is that we're tool builders. I read a study that measured the efficiency of locomotion for various species on the planet. The condor used the least energy to move a kilometer. And humans came in with a rather unimpressive showing about a third of the way down

> the list. It was not too proud of a showing for the crown of creation. . . . But then somebody at *Scientific American* had the insight to test the efficiency of locomotion for a man on a bicycle. And a man on a bicycle, or a human on a bicycle, blew the condor away—completely off the top of the charts.
>
> And that's what a computer is to me. . . . It's the most remarkable tool that we've ever come up with. . . . It's the equivalent of a bicycle for our minds.

Jobs's "bicycle for our minds" is a famous metaphor, and an artfully chosen one. The bicycle itself is a glorious achievement. Our ability to conceive, build, and ride one does indeed suggest, in Jobs's evocative phrase, that human beings are in some real sense "the crown of creation." The bicycle rider Jobs described could move faster than any other creature, but that person did not have superpowers—just real powers, efficiently and effectively channeled. In every way, including the powers it grants us, a bicycle is a perfectly personal thing.

Who wouldn't want a similar tool to extend the powers of our mind?

It is interesting to ask why Jobs chose such a humble metaphor. There are, after all, ways to travel considerably faster, farther, and with less expenditure of bodily energy than a bicycle. Why didn't Jobs go for more superpower mojo? What if he had said that a computer is a *motorcycle* for the mind or an *automobile* for the mind?

And since we are competing with the condor, why stop with terrestrial transportation? Why not say that the computer is an *airplane* for the mind? Or a *Saturn V rocket* for the mind?

But, in fact, if Jobs had used these metaphors, we might well feel at least a bit of discomfort. The airplane is firmly in the superpower zone; by the time we get to Saturn V rocket flight, we are in the realm of power that so outstrips human capabilities that such travel is a largely passive experience, harnessed to and controlled by cybernetic systems. These transportation technologies far transcend the traveler's agency and control.

Coming back to Earth, what if Jobs had compared a computer to a *self-driving car* for the mind? It would have been anachronistic to do so in 1991, yet this is much closer to what computers actually are—at least for the great majority of ordinary users. When I ride a bicycle, my inputs as the human operator (pedaling, steering, shifts in weight) have a fairly clear relation to the tool's behavior. But anyone who has helped a less computer-literate relative knows that this is not at all how it feels to operate a computer. The machine has a logic of its own. Often it is extremely difficult to know what it's doing, where it's going, or where it's taking us.

And then there is the subtle flattening of the dimensions of personhood implied in Jobs's choice of words. The computer might be "a bicycle for our minds," but is the computer a bicycle for our hearts? For our souls? It certainly does nothing to extend our strength. What makes riding a bicycle such a joyful experience, for five-year-olds and fifty-year-olds alike, is that it is an integrated experience, a heart-soul-mind-strength activity that computers rarely offer, whether in the 1990s or today.

Jobs's metaphor, then, turns out to be both beautiful and profoundly misleading. If he had chosen a more accurate metaphor, we might have had more mixed feelings about where computers were taking us.

But I believe Jobs's picture points us to a path less taken—a path to which we can still return.

There is a kind of technology that is easily distinguished from magic—a kind that involves us more and more deeply as persons rather than diminishing and sidelining us. This kind of technology elevates and dignifies human work, rather than reducing human beings to drones that do only the work the robots have not yet automated. It does not give us effortless power but instead gives us room to exert ourselves in deeper and more rewarding ways. This technology uses the abundant sources of energy (ideally renewable ones) available to us and the cybernetic control systems we have invented, not to replace people but to further involve them in creative work in the world.

This kind of technology is already in use, and we have almost all tasted its value—but because it does not advance the alchemists' dream, does not grant us superpowers, and does not as readily serve the interests of Mammon, it tends to be neglected and underdeveloped. Yet it is within reach, and in fact literally in the pocket, of most of the readers of this book.

RE-PLACING PERSONS

The philosopher Albert Borgmann used the word *devices* for the kind of technology that displaces earlier tools and, eventually, replaces the human beings who use them. The furnace in the basement replaces the hearth at the center of the home; the phonograph replaces the piano and the fiddle; the vacuum replaces the broom and is in turn replaced (almost) by the Roomba. But there is a way for technology to "replace" human beings in exactly the opposite sense. This kind of technology can re-place us, putting us back in our place as, in Jobs's words, "the crown of creation."

This kind of technology leads to the creation of cultural goods that are less like a device and more like a tool. Rather than disengaging us from the world and thrusting us into the superpower zone, this branch of technology relies on the ingenuity we human beings have brought to our work and play in the world from the very beginning. Yet this kind of technology has degrees of complexity, precision, and power that outstrip any pretechnological tool.

The best word for this kind of technology is *instruments*. And the fascinating thing about the computers that accompany us almost everywhere is that, though we call them "devices," they could just as well be instruments instead.

My wife, Catherine, is an experimental physicist, meaning that most of her working life has been located at the frontiers of both science and technology. In her postdoctoral work with Eric Mazur's lab at Harvard, Catherine and her colleagues used lasers to restructure materials at the nano scale. The black silicon pioneered by the Mazur lab has led to a new camera, the Aurora, that can produce full-color images with even the tiniest amount of available light. Other commercial applications in the future may include exquisitely accurate sensors and far more efficient solar cells.

As those new devices arrive, there may well be a rush of articles describing the new superpowers they will give us ("See in the dark!" "Generate power in the shade!"). Like so many devices before them, they may confer real benefits on humanity. Then they will soon fade into the background, another set of boring robots, leaving the most important things about us unaltered and undeveloped.

The creation of black silicon itself, however, looked nothing like the device paradigm. Devices promise to relieve us of effort and work and deliver almost instant results—but this discovery required painstaking, effortful work by whole teams of scientists over many years. The instruments and materials the inventors of black silicon built and used—lasers, electron microscopes, highly pure silicon chips, and more—certainly were high technology. Unlike a hammer or a nail, a laser and a chip of high-grade silicon are not something any human being can fashion or use by hand.

And yet they are not devices. They in no way replace human beings. They require a scientist to operate them, bringing the fullness of heart, soul, mind, and strength (because science, if done well, requires all these things) to the work of uncovering the beautiful order and abundance of the created world. The discoveries of the Mazur laboratory, and of labs all over the world in many different fields, emerge not because the researchers have superpowers but because they use instruments to focus and unleash genuinely human power. My wife would come home from her best days in the lab feeling the "good tired" that we feel after a day of flow—not reduced to enervated exhaustion like a person scaled back to a few repetitive motions or thoughts, but ready for the satisfied rest that comes when we have exerted ourselves toward one another and toward the world.

We use the word *instruments* in medicine and music as well, in a parallel way. Modern medicine depends on high technology, but much of that technology is used to better equip the person of the physician rather than replace or diminish them. Even the da Vinci Surgical System, approved by the FDA in 2000 and frequently described as a surgical robot, is not what we usually think of when we picture a robot. It has amazing capabilities, to be sure, extending surgeons' ability to reach inside the human body and remove entire organs through very small incisions. But it does not do anything on its own. It is just an instrument that assists human surgeons as they use their judgment and dexterity.

And then there are musical instruments, many of them technological achievements in their own right. Even a classical instrument like the grand piano became possible only with nineteenth-century technical advances, like the overstringing technique patented by Henry Steinway, Jr., in 1859. The piano was one of the first musical instruments to be turned into a musical device—something that played on its own with no skill required of its immediate operator—in the form of the player piano. But that device is gone, except as a curiosity in a few museums. The instrument remains, capable of enduring the pounding of two-year-olds and the agonized practice of six-year-olds, while still responding to the musicianship of sixteen-year-olds, seventy-six-year-olds, and anyone who kept practicing after they asked their parents if they could quit.

Every musical device in my family's home—from the click-wheel iPod we purchased in 2001 to the Bluetooth speaker we purchased last year—will be irretrievably obsolete within a generation and worthless in the money economy. But with reasonable care, the grand piano in our living room will survive to be pounded on, and perhaps practiced on, by my great-great-grandchildren. If the past hundred years are any guide, it may even be worth more in constant dollars than it is today.

YOU'LL NO LONGER HAVE TO, BUT YOU'LL NO LONGER BE ABLE TO

Every technical advance in human history has been borne on the wings of two promises:

1. "Now you'll be able to . . ."—The promise of expanding human experience and capacity in some way. You might not have studied piano as a child, the player-piano salesmen would say, but "now you'll be able to" have piano music in your home anyway.

2. "You'll no longer have to . . ."—The promise of relieving toil, drudgery, stress, and, for that matter, skill. "You'll no longer have to practice," says the player-piano brochure. "You'll no longer have to vacuum," says the Roomba review.

These promises—expanded capabilities, reduced burdens—accompanied even the most basic tools. The hammer promised that "now you'll be able to" fasten wood using iron nails that you could never drive in with your bare hands, while "you'll no longer have to" use more primitive techniques like binding wood together with cords of string or bark. But while tools are largely sold based on the first promise, it is the second promise that is the hallmark of our device-paradigm era. I bought a Roomba almost entirely because of its promise (not entirely fulfilled, alas) that I would "no longer have to" vacuum my living room, not because it greatly expanded the realm of "now you can."

There are two other consequences of any new device, however, that are far less often mentioned or observed because they are not drivers of sales and marketing. They are *restricted* capabilities and *enforced* burdens, and they

accompany "now you'll be able to" and "you'll no longer
have to" as surely as night follows day:

3. "You'll no longer *be able to* . . ."—The acquisition of this piece of technology will inevitably
shrink your capacity and experience in one dimension, often a creative dimension, even as it expands
it in the direction of consumption. Fill your home
with devices that play music, and the chance that
you will maintain the habits of practice that allow
you to make music yourself, to create rather than
consume, will shrink. Sign up for an unlimited
video-streaming service, and somehow the time
available for reading books—and concentrating on
them—will seem to dwindle.

4. "Now you'll *have* to . . ."—The new technology
will enforce new requirements, new behaviors, new
patterns of life, whether you wanted it to or not.
As I have learned to my chagrin, the music-making
devices we purchase, like the click-wheel iPod I
bought with such delight, come with a stiff "now
you'll have to upgrade" if we want to keep enjoying their benefits.

This bargain—the trade-offs we make between the
expansion of capacity and relief of burden, on the one
hand, and the diminishing of capacity and imposition of
burden, on the other hand—is not at all new. It goes back
to Plato's dialogue *Phaedrus,* in which Socrates retells

the story of Thoth inventing writing and presenting his invention to King Thamus. Thamus acknowledges that Thoth has done something very clever and that his invention will seem to give human beings more capacities. But, Thamus observes, Thoth's gift takes away capacities as well. (1) *Now you'll be able to* write down stories and information, meaning (2) y*ou'll no longer have to* remember them—true. But (3) *you'll no longer be able to* exercise the human capacity for oral memory, and (4) *now you'll have to* write something down in order to remember it.

It's amazing how often the *Phaedrus* is cited by the advocates of technology (especially, of course, information technology) as a way of dismissing critiques, as if the fact that worries about technology go back for thousands of years means that those worries are silly. To the contrary, it is clear that Socrates was exactly right about the trade-offs inherent in the widespread adoption of writing. Richard Bauckham's fascinating book *Jesus and the Eyewitnesses* marshals a wide range of evidence for how oral cultures develop an extraordinary ability in their members for committing long stretches of story and speech, verbatim, to memory. Most of us cannot imagine being able to hear a discourse once and then repeat it word for word. But such memorization was routine in Jesus' time and is still routine in oral cultures around the world today. For those of us embedded in a literate (or, increasingly, postliterate and image-based) culture, it is effectively inconceivable.

We may consider this trade between oral memory and

the vast expansion of written information to be worthwhile. But not all trades come on such favorable terms. And more importantly, not all technology demands such steep sacrifices. This is the crucial difference between tools, devices, and instruments.

Devices require us to accept a great deal of *you'll no longer be able to* and, increasingly, to accept a great deal of coerced behavior in the form of *now you'll have to* to access their promises of *now you'll be able to* and *you'll no longer have to*.

Instruments, on the other hand, are marvelously different. If devices promise relief of burdens and toil, the best instruments specialize in promise number one (*now you'll be able to*), even while they actually require a great deal of us. To *be able to* fashion black silicon required my wife and hundreds of other scientists to acquire advanced mathematical reasoning skills and manual dexterity—there was hardly any devicelike *you'll no longer have to* in the story of its invention.

But the best instruments also impose almost no cost in terms of promises (or threats) three and four. They expand the capacity of human beings without shrinking other parts of us at the same time. They do so because they extend our capacities by further developing our hearts, souls, minds, and strength—further involving us in the glorious and difficult work of being persons in the world.

So astronomers can use telescopes, even today's radio telescopes that are operated remotely by computers without a person ever having to visit the observatory itself, in ways that greatly expand the *now you'll be able to* understanding of our universe—and yet those telescopes, no matter how complex, in no way diminish astronomers' ability to step outside and gaze up at the stars, beholding them in all their complexity and furious beauty. In fact, what they have learned in the course of becoming astronomers will enable them to see, interpret, and understand the heavens far better than those of us who merely glance upward on a clear night. They use technology as an instrument, not a device.

In one of his essays, the writer Wendell Berry distinguishes between the path and the road. A path is the result of the traditional means of finding one's way through the world—a narrow, simple trail that blends into the landscape. A road, on the other hand, is imposed on the landscape by tools and technology. Paths are worn down over a long time; roads are built with whatever haste the budget can buy. Paths respond to the world, following the contours of the land; roads remake the world.

Paths and roads offer very different trade-offs among our four promises and threats. The path adds *now you'll be able to* (travel more easily from this place to this other place) while doing minimal damage in the form of *you'll no longer be able to*. It is not hard to go off a path if you see something worth visiting. But a road enforces a new kind of behavior. When driving on a road, it becomes more likely that *you'll no longer be able to* leave the road; even in a four-wheel-drive SUV, you are forced to travel along a single fixed route. That will be the case all the more should the road one day be dedicated to self-driving cars, when *you'll no longer have to* drive at all—which will also mean *you'll no longer be able to.*

The path expands what is possible, while foreclosing very little. But the road—in precise proportion to how technological it becomes—imposes severe costs of *you'll no longer be able to.* In some rural parts of the United States, on the entrance ramp to interstate highways, you will still see a picture of a horse behind the diagonal in a circle that internationally indicates exclusion. *You are no longer able to* ride a horse here, the sign says. Countless dimensions of human culture and history are excluded by the road.

Any reader of Wendell Berry gains a new appreciation for just how much *you'll no longer be able to* accompanies the promises of the modern world, and few consider Berry's arguments without wondering if we should simply roll back the whole modern project—if we could.

But perhaps there is another kind of path available to us. Perhaps it is not entirely too late to change course—not to reverse course, but to choose a different vision.

There is a recurring joke about the disappointments of the twenty-first century, especially among my fellow Gen Xers, that became the name of a Scottish indie rock band: We Were Promised Jetpacks. In their spirit, I suggest we take the late Steve Jobs at his word—because I think he was, in fact, sincere, and I think he was right.

We were promised a bicycle for the mind.

I suggest we hold out for what he promised and not let go until we have it.

We were not promised the disengagement and dullness of boring robots. We were not promised the addiction and anxiety of devices that tempt us with superpowers and leave us drained, that dangle hopes of satisfaction but leave us empty, that offer to recognize us but rob us of the face-to-face life for which we were made.

We were promised the fullness, the allness of life that we all experienced when we learned to ride on two wheels as children—the engagement of our bodies, the sharpening of our minds, the awakening of our hearts that we knew and longed for.

Just because we have ended up with computing devices does not mean we cannot expect, and even demand, that they become computing instruments instead.

The unique thing about computers is that they are general-purpose technology. A telescope will only ever be able to gather light from the sky—it cannot become a portrait camera or a piano. But my iPhone, held up on a winter's night outdoors, can name the constellations for me, helping me see the sky in a new way. With the right software it could equip a professional astronomer with powerful analytical tools to explore still-unsolved mysteries of our cosmos. It can also allow me to make images using its lens and processing power, while enabling a practiced photographer to make images that could endure for centuries as art. It can provide the recording apparatus needed to capture one of my own semiprofessional musical performances, and, in the hands of a skilled producer and musician, it could make music for the ages. Because it is, in the end, simply a blank screen that responds to human touch, with the right software it can become the ultimate instrument for any number of exercises of personal heart, soul, mind, and strength.

Or, of course, it can serve as the ultimate device. It can occupy me late into the night so that I never even go outdoors and look up at the sky; it can present me with endlessly consumable images so that I never make an image of my own or make only those that slot easily into the template of Mammon's and magic's world; it can play music for me from my first day to my last without my ever learning to play.

It would not be quite right to say that it is entirely up to me whether my iPhone, or future computational technology yet to be developed, becomes an instrument or a device—although it is true enough that every day I can choose which way to use it, within the limits of the programs and interfaces that others have designed it to provide.

But it is certainly true that in the long run that choice is up to *us:* what we ask our technology to do, what we ask its designers to optimize, what we believe is the good life that we are pursuing together.

INSTRUMENTS OF CARE

My friend Jessica Nam Kim is a serial entrepreneur with three start-ups to her credit, starting with the baking company she launched in college. She had built her most recent firm, which made innovative activity kits that children and parents could enjoy together, to the point of a successful sale and exit from the business. Like any good entrepreneur, she pondered her next move with a dozen different ideas jostling for attention in her head.

And then her mother's pancreatic cancer, which had been in remission, came back for the final time.

Everything stopped for Jessica as her mother and father moved in with her own young family, rejoining their household in the most intimate way. Jessica and her father cared for her mother during the months when treatment seemed possible. They kept doing so during the months when the options for treatment were one by one set aside, then during the final weeks when technology could do no more than limit her mother's suffering. Through it all, they provided the love and presence her mother needed until her dying breath.

Rocked by the loss of the one who had given birth to her and nursed her, the grandmother of her own children, the wife of her now-bereaved father, Jessica spent days and weeks simply in the grip of grief.

But she also was reflecting, paying attention, discovering, and, without even knowing it, designing.

She reflected on the overwhelming number of choices

she had had to make while caring for her mother, and the fragmentary guidance and support she'd gotten from a medical system that is expert at delivering drugs and surgeries but not always designed to deliver real care.

Jessica started wondering what role, if any, technology could play in the most important part of any suffering person's life: not the medicines or treatments but the other people who come around them and provide the care they cannot provide for themselves. She discovered, as she talked to more and more people who had been caregivers, how much their lives careened between the well-intentioned but vague offers of help from countless friends and a sense of being utterly alone in navigating the complexities of illness and dying.

As the grief of her mother's death settled deep into Jessica's heart and body, an idea began to form, not displacing the grief but growing out of its soil—the idea of bending the technology of social media into an instrument of care at life's extremities. She read vigorously, began sketching ideas, iterating, discarding, refining. She recruited Steven Lee to be a co-founder. Steven brought deep technical and operational skills and also, along with his family, had cared for his grandfather over many years of Parkinson's disease. They started talking to investors about a different kind of app.

This app, rather than scaling up to large, impersonal audiences, would facilitate a small circle of support from close family, friends, and neighbors that caregivers depend on. Jessica developed convictions about the kind of advertising such an app would never take, the kinds of reward systems it would never activate, the kinds of superpowers it would not promise—and also about how the right technology could actually strengthen the thin relationships of those caring for the most vulnerable, helping them become thicker paths of meaningful action.

In July 2019, Jessica, Steven, and their team launched ianacare. In the first year after launch, it quickly grew to serve 250,000 families facing life-altering conditions ranging from disability to terminal illness. Ianacare helps a whole community offer support in concrete and meaningful ways, assisting with decisions that so easily become overwhelming amid the daily work of feeding, bathing, holding, and waiting.

Its name, ianacare, comes from the four words that Jessica realized she had most needed during her long days of caring for her dying mother—the four words every caregiver most needs. They are, in fact, the four words every one of us most needs in life—the words that magic and Mammon will never speak, the words that a truly personal technology could restore.

The four words are "I am not alone."

FROM FAMILY TO HOUSEHOLD

Living Together as Persons

One way to understand what we are most missing in Mammon's empire, and what we can and should rebuild, is to ask, What kind of place do we require to thrive as persons?

If you and I are heart-soul-mind-strength complexes designed for love, we need a place where we can exercise our fundamental capacities—a place where we can channel our emotions and longings, be known in our unique depth of self, contribute to understanding and interpreting the world, and apply our bodies' strength and agility to worthwhile work in all three planes of physical reality. Above all, we need a place where we can invest ourselves deeply in others, come to care about their flourishing, and give ourselves away in mutual service and sacrifice in ways that secure our own identities instead of erasing them.

The name for this kind of place, I have come to believe, is the *household*.

This old, slightly musty word is the best option we have in English for something that was central to life in the ancient world and is still central to life in many cultures today. A household is both place and people—or maybe better, it is a particular people with a particular place. A household is a community of persons who may well take shelter under one roof but also and more fundamentally take shelter under one another's care and concern. They provide for one another, and they depend on one another. They mingle their assets and their liabilities, their gifts and their vulnerabilities, in such a way that it is hard to tell where one member's end and another member's begin.

The household is the fundamental community of persons. Built on more than an isolated pair but encompassing few enough people that all can be deeply and truly and persistently noticed and seen, the household is perfectly sized for the recognition we all were looking for the moment we were born.

It might seem that the more appropriate word for such a community would be *family*. But while they are frequently intertwined, the household is fundamental for personhood in a way that family actually is not, in two ways.

First, family extends beyond households. My cousin

Tom, who lives in another region of the United States, is a member of my family, but we have never been members of the same household. Likewise, I left my parents' household many years ago, but they are still very much my family. As valuable as these relationships are, they are not the same, for the purposes of flourishing as persons, as the day-to-day life together that is the essence of a household.

Second, and maybe even more important, households extend beyond family. This was true in the Greco-Roman world, where the Latin word *familia* meant something closer to what *household* means for us. A household would include those not directly related to the *paterfamilias* by blood or marriage but connected to him by various kinds of dependence. Indeed, though we do not have Greco-Roman-style households today in the West, there are many cultures that do, though they too often perpetuate some of that world's most violent and violating features—above all enslavement, which is still a de facto reality in parts of our world, along with absolute patriarchy.

But households that extend beyond family, built on bonds of love, are more possible and more common than we often realize. Before getting married, I had lived for several years with four men. Seeking an intentional common life, for most of that time we had a single bank account, into which we deposited all our income and out of which we paid all our expenses. For the first four years of marriage, my wife and I lived under one roof with several other housemates, both married and unmarried. I finished the manuscript of this book as a guest at Coram Deo, a building in New York City where two married couples and their children live full-time. They provide hospitality to travelers, an environment of Christian worship and prayer, and working space for several ministries and businesses—combining, much as Gaius's household might have done, the daily rhythms of family life with church services and daily commerce.

This quality of households—the way they extend beyond family formed by birth or marriage—is especially important because it means that, unlike family, households are places where every person can find a home. Widows and especially orphans have lost crucial members of their families, but they can and should be welcomed into households. Some people have outlived or been separated from all the family they know in the world, but they can still be members of a household. In our modern world, the demographic reality is that many people will never marry, but that doesn't mean they cannot join a household.

How do you know if you're part of a household?

You are part of a household if there is someone who knows where you are today and who has at least some sense of how it feels to be where you are. You are part of a household if there is someone who moves more quietly when they know you are asleep. You are part of a household if someone would check on you if you did not awaken.

You are part of a household if people know things about you that you do not know about yourself, including things that if you did know you would seek to hide. You are part of a household if others are close enough to see you and know you as well as, or better than, you know yourself.

You are part of a household if you experience the conflict that is the inevitable companion of closeness—if someone else makes such demands on you that you sometimes fantasize about driving them out of your life. You are part of a household if you sometimes dream of running away, perhaps to a far country, so that you will not be so terribly well known.

You are part of a household if your return from a long journey prompts a spontaneous celebration. You are part of a household if, when you avoid a party because of your anger, pride, guilt, or shame, someone notices and comes outside to plead with you to come in.

This is the one thing we need more than any other: a community of recognition. While we must always insist that every human being is a person whether or not they are seen or treated as one by others, we also know that no human being can *flourish* as a person unless they are seen and treated as one. And for that, the household is the first and best place.

We need a place where we cannot hide. We need a place where we cannot get lost.

So much of the tragedy of the modern world comes down to this: Most of us do not have such a place. Perhaps we once did, for a time. Maybe there was a home down the street, belonging to extended family or friends, whose back door was always open to us when we were a child; tastes of life under one roof that came with military service or short-term mission work; a year or two with roommates who did more together than just split the household bills. But because these arrangements are not expected to last, they readily dissolve.

Many of us have friends, but friendships that are not bound together by household life tend to remain thin and fragile in our mobile world—all the more so after the peak bonding years of late adolescence. Many of us have families, but family is fragile, too, and its most crucial stage—the raising of children from infancy to young adulthood—is temporary by design. A married couple with one or two children at home is the implicit cultural norm, but today it describes only a minority of the households identified by the United States census. And such a small family is barely large enough to really form the kind of community of personhood for which we are made, even before the children are grown and gone.

If you are looking for a single proximate cause of the loneliness that is epidemic in our world, it is the dearth of households.

In my judgment this is even more consequential than the decline in family life per se, though the two are related in complex ways. It is certainly true that we are witnessing something close to a collapse in both marriage and childbearing in the "Western" world (that is, the Mammon-driven world, the world where technology has most reshaped our imagination). And it is also true that even in cultures where households extend well beyond kin, like Gaius's Greco Roman world or Indian Brahmin families with multiple servants, households still are most often built—and certainly tend to be most stable when built—on marriage and childbearing.

So the household cannot be a direct replacement for the family, and households are most likely to form and last when they are connected to families. But families thrive best when they are part of households. The "nuclear" family is as fissile as its name suggests. Without participation in a broader network of kin and friendship, and especially under the pressures of consumer culture, few marriages and families thrive.

THE SACRIFICIAL HOUSEHOLD

If we want to follow a different way from the way of Mammon, we need to begin by building households. Like anything really worthwhile, this is not easy. Indeed, it goes against almost everything that magic and Mammon have trained us to want. To live in a household is to give up a great deal of autonomy and independence—the very things that make us desperately lonely but also the very things that we believe are our birthright as subjects of Mammon's empire.

The household, with its proximity, interdependence,

and various kinds of intimacy, limits the freedom of its members in real ways—not least the individual sexual freedom prized by emerging adults in much of the Western world. At the same time, the household challenges the still-powerful ideal of the bourgeois family, the cozy nuclear family unit insulated, at least in their home, from visibility and duty to others. Middle-class adults value financial freedom—the ability to spend our money in ways that we see fit, without accountability or the challenge of providing radically for the needs of others close to us. These shallow freedoms are hard to find in a household.

The sacrifice of autonomy and invisibility—the choice to depend on others and be seen by others—seems like a steep price to pay for those of us shaped by Mammon's promises. Like the younger son in Jesus' parable, we are powerfully tempted to cash out of our original household, taking in cash what we previously had only in trust. This is the very heart of Mammon's bargain, its foul and foolish invitation to make ourselves independent. The funds run out much sooner than we expect, and the abundance we expected is hollow even before the money is gone.

But for every prodigal who builds a life of fragile freedom from the entanglements of household life, there are countless more who are desperate to find a home. Among them are the 120,000 children waiting for adoption in the United States alone and the 20,000 children who age out of the foster care system in our country each year as they become legal adults. Also among these prodigals are many of the winners of our meritocratic world, the college graduates who move to cities and advance professionally while living in studio apartments and swiping through profiles on Tinder, as well as the millions of migrant workers who follow the fickle seasons and shifts in labor markets, trying to eke out enough income to send to family far away. And then there are so many who reach the end of their lives, even lives that had once been full of family and neighbors, living alone or in institutional environments, barely named and barely known.

There are all kinds of palliatives that can dull the pain of our household-less world, but nothing can truly erase the fact that most of us live long stretches of our lives without the community of recognition we most need. And it should go without saying that merely having roommates—or a spouse or parents or children—is no guarantee at all, in Mammon's realm, that we will be members of real communities of recognition, that there will be anyone who really knows us.

The more successful we have been on Mammon's terms, the more likely we are to aspire to houses with multiple individual bedrooms—even for children and adolescents, who most need tireless attention and support. We fill those rooms with devices that provide just enough simulation of recognition and stimulation of entertainment to dull our real need and prevent us from seeking one another out. Of course, a room of one's own can be a real gift, and the ability to be alone is part of a healthy personal life (in the close quarters of a household, solitude is one of the many things we have to sacrificially provide for one another). But for some people, the quiet of a room of one's own has turned into the isolation of a screen of one's own. Even when we are in the same room, we may rarely fully see and be seen by another face.

SOCIAL ARCHITECTURE

So our next redemptive move for Mammon's empire will be to begin redesigning our lives to be more and more household-like.

If you live with others, are there times in every day when you are together, building the fabric of a life in which you are seen and known? Are you engaged in heart-soul-mind-strength activities together, creating and not just consuming—in the kitchen, in the living room, in the garage, in the yard, or on the porch? Are there parts of your daily life where different members of the household contribute in ways that merge your gifts and needs, strengths and weaknesses? Or are you, even if technically family, more like mere roommates, with each one cooking, cleaning, and caring for themselves? Are there ways you can provide for one another rather than assuming that each person will provide for themselves?

In some homes the obvious answer to all these questions will already be *yes*—but in others these questions can prompt significant redesigning of the patterns of daily life, from who does the dishes (and who does whose dishes, and how many people do the dishes) to whether the whole household sits down for dinner or goes outside for a daily walk.

And then who needs to be included in these household practices—who needs to be invited further in? Do others have the key to your house and an open invitation to use it? Could family members who currently live at a comfortable distance be invited to a more uncomfortable but also more recognition-friendly proximity? The coronavirus lockdowns of 2020, with their restrictions on school and childcare, led many families to create pods or umbrellas that covered a handful of parent-and-child units. How could those kinds of mutual relationships continue even when the lockdowns are past?

Even to raise these questions, at least for me and my house, is to raise a whole set of doubts and fears. Whom do I really trust enough to invite this close to my own life, my spouse, my children? How will I keep the sense of privacy and untroubled autonomy that I have come to prize? What risks will I be adding to my life if I invite people in closer than arm's length, if I become dependent on others rather than exchanging payment for services that leave me formally unentangled? What will happen if I start giving more and gifting less?

But the truth is that only by pressing through and beyond these questions will we ever grow to have people we can trust outside our tightest inner circle. The privacy we cherish is in constant danger of curdling into isolation. Even a few adverse events in our marriage or personal health, let alone the march of years and aging, could tip our current independence into terminal loneliness.

We can begin to change the social architecture of our lives simply by asking these questions and pursuing the possibilities they awaken. But this will naturally begin to shape physical architecture as well. Much of America's built environment, especially our residential settings, is poorly designed for real, personal life. Houses that would have seemed like a sprawling villa to Gaius, with square footage capable of supporting a household of twenty or more, are designed in ways that make them viable housing for just a handful of people. Zoning codes in many towns prohibit groups of nonrelated individuals from living under the same single-family roof.

When we leave our homes, we have too many roads (which the urban development organization Strong Towns defines as "a high-speed route between productive places") and not enough streets ("a place where people interact with businesses and residences, and where wealth is produced"). Worst of all, we are plagued, especially in the United States, with "stroads"—the distinctively American development that locates shopping, entertainment, and churches not on person-scale streets where they could be part of a thriving, diverse heart-soul-mind-strength environment, but on wide, car-scale roads that isolate each building from the next, one parking lot at a time.

All this calls out for redesign, and there are vanguard movements like the "co-housing" movement that have built new kinds of communities, mostly on a small scale, starting from the assumption that we want a more household-friendly way of life. (The "new urbanism" of the last few decades, which addressed some of the deficiencies of suburban living, often left assumptions about household size and autonomy largely intact.) Cities like Portland, Oregon, and Austin, Texas, partly prompted by runaway housing costs, have revised their zoning to allow small cottages to be added to existing lots, facilitating intergenerational housing or guest renters who could easily become part of existing households.

Deep cultural change ultimately must shape the built environment, and mere changes in physical architecture are less important, initially, than a change in our imagination—the good life we believe we are seeking. Without a thorough repudiation of the promises of magic and Mammon, even genuine quests for a renewed kind of community can be hijacked. The co-working firm WeWork, which had a meteoric rise in the 2010s, got so much right. We do want to work in flexible and beautiful spaces; we do want a work environment that treats us as heart-soul-mind-strength realities (through attention to design, different kinds of seating for the different moods and rhythms of the workday, yoga classes, and good coffee). WeWork did not invent the mobile office with flexible lease terms; what it did was take sterile corporate environments and make them quasi-personal. It was so close to the kind of places we were meant for.

But in the realm of persons, *so close* is not at all close

enough. What WeWork was not, and could not be, was a household: a place where persons live together under a canopy of trust rather than transaction. I would much rather work in a WeWork-type space than in the Regus lounges that were the only viable alternative in the 1990s and 2000s. But at least the Regus space did not pretend to be anything other than a transactional environment. In spite of WeWork's distressed-wood and free-flowing handwritten signs, it was not a sustainable, communal effort in rebuilding a more personal life—it was a highly leveraged short-to-long-term-lease-arbitrage business with shaky financial underpinnings that nearly collapsed, was forced to abruptly lay off thousands of employees, and yet somehow managed to make a billionaire of its founder on his way out the door.

Given the choice between a fairly sterile environment that doesn't pretend to be anything but a place for business and a simulation of the beloved community that masks unsustainable exploitation, I'll personally take the Regus. But what we need, and what we are hungering for, is the real thing.

THE CANOPY OF COMMUNITY

The sociologist Peter Berger wrote an influential book about the sociology of religion called *The Sacred Canopy*. To borrow his metaphor, I have come to believe that all truly personal life has to take place under a canopy—

a kind of umbrella under which we shelter and can let down our guard. The most important contribution the household makes is sending into the wider world persons who know what it is to live under a canopy of trust.

Trust is the heart of life together in community because it is the heart of creativity. All creative endeavors involve risk. The greatest creative endeavor of all—the begetting, birthing, and raising of children—involves the greatest risk, but any venture away from the predictable and known exposes us to the possibility of loss. To genuinely extend ourselves in the world requires us to have someone bearing risk along with us. That is what trust provides.

Take away trust, and all you have left is coercion—the power of the strongest to compel the obedience of the rest. But coercion is a brittle and barren resource because ultimately there is very little good that I can force you to do. Human communities, all the way up to empires, thrive only to the extent that they can draw on something more than force, something that unleashes personal energy and creativity to discover and create lasting value in the world.

We instinctively feel when the canopy over our heads is torn. You may stop for fuel or a sandwich in a part of a city where crime is an element of daily life. The person serving you is behind a bulletproof wall of plexiglass, almost entirely cut off from real recognition or conversation. They are shielded from the vulnerability of not knowing who will come into the store next, with what requirements and what weapons; but you, on the other side of the barrier, also know that should someone come into the shop with intentions of violence, the employee will not share your vulnerability. At best they might place a call for help to distant and uninterested officials. You are technically in their presence, but you are not under their canopy of trust—you feel in your gut that you are alone in all the ways that really matter.

You will feel this even on a short visit. But grow up in this environment, spending all the formative years of your life in it, and your very epigenetics, the expression of your genes, will be shaped by the constant vigilance that comes from knowing that you are on your own, that your neighborhood is on its own, that your people are on their own, unprotected and unrecognized as sacred. No wonder you will turn to any community, no matter how violent it may be toward outsiders, if it promises to take you under its canopy of trust.

Canopies of trust can be small and temporary. I meet with someone I know only through mutual friends. We sit under a small canopy for an hour or so, meeting at a coffee shop that creates a space where conversation is welcomed and strangers can interact as if they were already friends. Holding up the canopy is the fact that we both arrived reasonably on time or made a sincere apology if we were late; that we will both leave at roughly the time we had agreed on beforehand; that we take turns in the conversation, listening and speaking in an exchange of attention and regard. But as we leave the coffee shop, the canopy that has held us together dissolves as we go our separate ways in the world.

Fruitful lives take shape under a cascade of canopies, each larger and more enduring than the one before. I go back from the coffee shop to my office, where I work with a team each day. We collaborate under the canopy of employment, meaning that we do not have to renegotiate our terms of engagement each day, as gig workers would have to do. Deeper forms of creative work are possible—work that requires more time, more energy, more risk. The canopy above us is not infinite—we are a firm, after all, not a family. Our jobs are not guaranteed, and our employment is not for life. But we do work, this day, week, month, and quarter, under a canopy of trust that frees us to accomplish things together that we could never accomplish alone.

And that firm, in turn, relies on other canopies above it—the political canopies of city and nation; the canopies of trust and truthfulness provided by bookkeeping, accounting, and audits; and the canopy of markets where buyers and sellers come together in honest and free exchanges of value. None of these happen by accident. All of them had to be built at some point in the past, all of them have to be maintained in the present, and none of them can be taken for granted in the future. Indeed, we live in a time when many people no longer believe those canopies of trust exist at all, or ever existed in the first place—a time when many of them are being torn by suspicion and betrayal. The whole world rediscovered in 2020 how much our lives depend on being able to breathe the air around us without fear of infection. But trust is the oxygen of any healthy social world. We are all discovering how a failure of any of the canopies that cover our common life leaves us unable to breathe.

There is no easy way to repair these canopies once they are torn, but if there is a place where we learn to establish them, it is within family and in households that treat their members like family. The household is the first and most important canopy of trust we need to thrive as human beings—a place where we can always go, a place where we are safe enough to sleep.

BENEATH THE CANOPY OF THE SKY

Any place where there is trust will, sooner or later, become a place where there is disappointment, if not betrayal. The parable we often call the parable of the prodigal son is actually the story of an entire household, and it is a story of a canopy of trust torn, mended, and then torn again. The father, the elder son, and the servants witness the younger brother demanding to cash out of that household's canopy of trust, carrying off his share of the family's common wealth in bags of money; but then those same servants witness the elder brother refusing to receive and restore his heartbroken and humbled younger brother, refusing to join the redemption and resurrection party under their father's roof.

We will not live in any household without discovering our own capacities for betrayal, selfishness, and self-righteousness. But it is also in the household that we can discover our capacities for humility, repentance, and forgiveness—can embrace one another again and plead for one another to come in again. Indeed, given our fallen nature, it is through these very experiences of rupture and repair, of tearing and reweaving the canopy, that we actually learn how to become people who can trust and people who are trustworthy. If we do not learn and practice these things in our households, it is exceedingly unlikely that we will be able to build the social canopies of markets, cities, and nations under which others can shelter as well.

To build these kinds of households requires the very opposite of magic. It is work that is patient, humble, and slow. And these households produce the very opposite of Mammon, with its fraudulent promise of abundance without dependence. They create, through mutual dependence, the kind of abundance that cannot be counted or carted away and that does not rust and cannot be stolen.

To rebuild households would begin to undermine Mammon itself. If we lived this way together, we would begin to fundamentally change our economy in the most literal sense and eventually change the structure of economic life more broadly—what we value, measure, and reward. To begin this kind of economic restoration does not require us to change the practices of Wall Street, the

Federal Reserve, or the European Central Bank—or even to know, exactly, what ought to replace them. We just (just!) have to redirect our energies away from Mammon's domain and turn toward a realm where Mammon has nothing to offer. And then we need to invite others to join us under that new shelter.

FROM CHARMED TO BLESSED

The Community of the Unuseful

On an April night in 2013, I drove away from my friend David Sacks's home, having seen him alive for the last time. At forty-five years old, with four children under the age of ten, he was dying of cancer. We would bury him a few days later, closing one chapter in a relationship that was one of the great unearned gifts of my life.

There were a few untroubled years of friendship with David and his wife, Angie—the days when David was not yet terminally ill and would routinely and effortlessly beat me at squash. Then, the strangely joy-filled months after his diagnosis, as a schedule of drastic drugs held back the worst of the disease. During those months we watched our favorite movies together—David especially insisted

that we watch Terrence Malick's *The Thin Red Line*—
and tried to fit a lifetime of conversation into the days we
had left. Then came his last days, David weak and largely
silent on his bed as a few of us gathered, waited, prayed,
and sang.

I drove the one mile between David's home and ours
several nights during that last week of his life. Some nights
I shouted and cursed at God; some nights I was spent
and still. But the last night as I drove away, it dawned
on me that there was only one word that could really
capture the fullness of what we were experiencing. That
word was *blessing*.

At first, the thought struck me as strange. This word—
and its Instagram hashtag cousin #blessed—has come to
be used for moments of peak delight and, frankly, peak
privilege. What I was experiencing and witnessing was
nothing like that. My friend was dying. His wife was
about to be a widow; his children were about to lose
their father. His life, which had been the very picture of
creative love, was being cut short in the midst of all the
good he had done and could do.

Yet God was mysteriously but undeniably present that
week. Love was tangible, direct, and practical. Life was
raw but also real, in a way that those of us who live in the
Bubble Wrap of affluence so rarely experience.

Blessing shows up again and again in the Hebrew
Scriptures. In many of the most consequential instances,
someone is dying—or about to be born. Isaac and Jacob
each bless their sons from their deathbed. In Deuter-

onomy Moses lays out God's blessings—and curses—for God's people as they are on the threshold of the Promised Land and Moses is on the threshold of his departure from this world. Elijah blesses Elisha moments before the bewildering whirlwind carries him away forever.

And then, in the New Testament, the first person to be blessed is a young woman who is told, in practically the same breath as the announcement of divine favor, that a sword will pierce her heart. Her son pronounces blessings ("beatitudes") for the meek, the poor, the hungry, the persecuted. But in the version of the beatitudes found in Luke, he also calls down curses for the rich, the well fed, the satisfied—the very ones who might well tag themselves #blessed.

That final week of David's life caused me to reconsider the relative absence of suffering in my own story. What had I missed, I wondered, by never before being invited so close to someone's deathbed? The only other person I had visited in their very final days was my maternal grandmother. She lay on her bed just around the corner from the formal living room with the piano, where I sat at her request and played hymn after hymn. Then, with me still sitting at the piano, out of sight but not out of earshot, we began to speak in a way we had never spoken before—of God and his goodness, of regret and forgiveness, of loss and hope. In her soft southern accent she spoke of her love and pride in me—my last blessing from her—and then fell into fitful sleep. I left for the North the next morning knowing we would not see each other again, and somehow all was well.

This was blessing—being present with another in the Presence of Another, the gift of promise in the midst of grief.

It was not, and is not, the dominant note of my life—though I hope in the end it will be.

SMALLER THAN BLESSED

Most of my life has been something much smaller than *blessed*. My life has been *charmed*.

Charmed is a pagan word, a magical word, a word from fairy tales. To be charmed is to be magically held apart from harm, endowed for a time with a bubble of prosperity and power. For one evening, Cinderella is charmed. Aladdin's lamp is charmed, as long as he has wishes left. The sorcerer's apprentice, for a few hours, manages to charm the broom.

Much of what gets tagged #blessed should be tagged #charmed instead. Youth is a charm. Beauty is a charm. Words and numbers came easily to me in childhood— I found myself "good" at school, in a way that deceived me so deeply for so long about what it meant to be truly "good." That, too, was a charm.

Well into my forties I had lived this kind of life. I had evaded or escaped the extraordinary afflictions, and almost all the ordinary ones, that most of humanity suffers, in ways that would seem to most of my fellow human beings ridiculously fortunate, the result of the capricious favor of some genie or god. So, in many ways, had my friend David before his illness. Part of what had drawn me into friendship with him, if I am honest, was the prospect that draws so many of us into friendship with people who are unusually attractive and fortunate—the chance to step inside a charmed circle and experience the lightness and possibility that seem to be found there.

There is a slippery relationship between being charmed and being blessed, one that God's own people seem to struggle to work out. Jacob, who comes out of the womb grabbing on to his brother's heel, ultimately steals the blessing, posing as his elder brother before his blinded father. He clearly sees his father's blessing as something with a kind of talismanic power, as does the rest of his family when the deceit is discovered. It will now be Jacob, not Esau, who lives whatever kind of charmed life his father is able to impart by way of both words and gifts.

But later, when Jacob and Esau are about to meet again after many years of estrangement, comes the defining event of Jacob's story, an all-night wrestling match with a foe who is more than an angel. No trick, magic or otherwise, works with this adversary—it neither tires nor relents—yet Jacob keeps even in the hand-to-hand battle. As dawn breaks, his opponent simply touches Jacob on his hip and it is dislocated. Now Jacob is hanging on for dear life, with just one request: "I will not let go until you bless me."

He leaves the predawn wrestling match with two things: a permanent limp and a new name. That name, Israel, is a capacious word that could mean, as the text suggests, one who manages to prevail over God—but it also can mean one who contends with God, or one with whom God contends. What it surely does not mean— what you cannot possibly think it means if you know the story of the people called Israel—is one who is charmed by God.

In the story of blessing there is no magic. But in the story of magic there is no blessing, either. Charms are not just unpredictable and arbitrary; fairy tales remind us over and over that they are temporary. And when they are withdrawn, even with advance notice, like Cinderella's carriage turning into a pumpkin at midnight, their effects vanish. Perhaps, as with Cinderella, they have given us just enough time at the ball to have a chance at real love.

THE HOUSEHOLD OF THE DISPOSSESSED

My friends Mel and Dave Murray met at a Christian college in Arkansas. The photos from their college years show them much as they are today: both strikingly attractive—charming, you might well say—though if you look closely, you see an extra quality in both of their eyes, a combination of wonder and sadness.

When I met them for the first time, they were living in the city of Dehradun, India, where they had started two entrepreneurial ventures. Mel was leading the fashion brand Joyn, which makes accessories sold in high-end boutiques around the world, using high-quality leather and artisanally printed fabrics. More unconventionally, Dave had founded one of the world's premier makers of custom acoustic guitars.

Both businesses employed persons who had lived distinctly uncharmed lives. Because of addiction, illness, caste, or gender, the society around them had marked them as unworthy of respect and opportunity. But Mel and Dave hired them, and these very persons became makers of some of the finest and most beautiful cultural goods you will ever see. Or, in the case of the Dehradun Guitar Company, not just see but also hear.

The government of India has become more suspicious of Western residents in recent years, especially those who profess Christian faith. In 2018, after five years of life in Dehradun, the Murrays and their children were required to leave the country practically overnight, with no assurance of ever being able to return. Instead of moving back to the United States, they went to northern Thailand, near the Myanmar border. There they continued to live among the materially poor and launched a new venture, JoyCorps, which helps incubate artisanal businesses all over South Asia.

Dave and Mel had many losses to grieve in their sudden move. Among the greatest for Mel was a community ten minutes from their home in Dehradun. She had been looking for a source of handmade fabric when she heard that there was a leper colony that had taught the women living there to weave. She did find fabric there, of high quality. But she also found something of far greater value.

The characteristic effect of leprosy is damage to the extremities—fingers and toes, and eventually hands and feet, but also the nose. Sufferers endure not just disability but disfigured bodies—above all, faces. For millennia the disease has been a byword for contagion and a reason for exclusion. We now know that it is by no means highly contagious, but traditional societies still deal with leprosy by casting its sufferers out. In Dehradun, Sister Agnes Kunze had created a community for them, inspired by the woman we remember as Saint Teresa of Calcutta.

It was a household of the dispossessed. "They were completely cast out, with no rights," Mel told me. "But inside the community, they were making beautiful things with their hands, though some of them were weaving with six or seven digits missing. Outside the door of their community, they had no value—but inside they had incredible value."

Inside those doors, Mel found a place unlike any other. "I walked in, and I felt like I was in a piece of heaven. It was beautiful—communal—light, bright, with no heaviness. It became one of the places I would visit on my hard days, when India was really tough."

Wherever they go, Mel and Dave find themselves living among those who suffer. "We had in our community twenty individuals who were polio victims, quite a few with schizophrenia, four who were autistic, one who was both blind and deaf. Our friends from the United States would ask us what it was like to move into a community of such great need, where people needed so much from us. But that's all wrong. We needed one another—if only to remind one another that we need the grace of God to offer anything to the world.

"I told someone that I felt like I had met Jesus for the first time there, and she became quite offended. 'You've known Jesus since you were a young girl,' she said. And I have. But we get to know Jesus through his body. He calls us his body—can you believe that? If we are not with those who are suffering, we are literally missing a piece of the body of Christ. I came to know more of him when I was with those who were part of his body."

THOSE WHO CANNOT SERVE MAMMON

The shortest letter of Paul in the New Testament is one of the most superficially troubling and also one of the most deeply revolutionary. In it Paul sends a runaway slave back to his master, Paul's friend Philemon. The slave, Onesimus, gives us one more example of the terribly practical naming habits of the ancient world, as his name simply means "useful." From his very birth he had been marked out to be a coin in others' economy. We do not know the circumstances under which he ran away, but we know that, like others, he would have attempted to eke out an existence in the busy anonymity of a large city, perhaps Corinth or Colossae.

There, somehow, he met Paul. Normally, this would mean a runaway slave's worst nightmare had come true:

a friend and equal of his *paterfamilias* had met him, had recognized who his master was, and was sending him home. Such a return was usually the occasion for horrific violence. Slaves who had run away and been caught were often tattooed on the face with the words "Stop me, I am a runaway" so that they could never run away again.

But Paul was different. Paul was himself by this point a prisoner of Rome, meaning he, too, had been marked out as someone of minimal value, a threat to Caesar's empire rather than a resource for it. And Paul, who had been born free, now freely called himself a "servant of Jesus Christ" (Rom. 1:1—using the same word, *doulos,* that would have been used to describe Onesimus). Through Paul, Onesimus had come to know the crucified and risen Jesus as his own Lord and Savior—or, as Paul put it, Onesimus was Paul's own "child . . . whose father I have become during my imprisonment" (Philem. 1:10).

And so Paul sent Onesimus back to his friend Philemon with a letter tucked under his arm.

Playing on Onesimus's name, Paul wrote, "Formerly he was useless to you"—presumably by running away—"but now he is indeed useful both to you and to me" (verse 11). And then comes this extraordinary sequence:

> I am sending him, that is, my own heart, back to you. I wanted to keep him with me, so that he might be of service to me in your place during my imprisonment for the gospel; but I preferred to do nothing without your consent, in order

that your good deed might be voluntary and
not something forced. Perhaps this is the reason
he was separated from you for a while, so that
you might have him back forever, no longer as a
slave but more than a slave, a beloved brother—
especially to me but how much more to you,
both in the flesh and in the Lord.

So if you consider me your partner, welcome
him as you would welcome me. (Verses 12–17)

Let us ponder how Paul describes Onesimus in this
compact masterpiece of persuasion. The runaway slave—
the "useful" one who had become "useless," as worthless
as a piece of broken pottery, is now (1) doubly useful,
and indeed (2) could have sacrificially taken the place of
Philemon himself in caring for Paul during his imprisonment. But Onesimus is by no means treated by Paul
simply as a valuable servant, nor would Paul have him be
treated as such by Philemon. Rather than keeping him,
Paul wishes him to be a member of Philemon's household again, welcomed back (3) "no longer as a slave"
but (4) "more than a slave," indeed (5) as a "beloved
brother," treated as such (6) "in the flesh"—that is, as
a biological brother, literal kin—as well as (7) "in the
Lord"—honored as a member of the family of Jesus
himself—and (8) to be welcomed in precisely the way a
"partner" would be welcomed.

There may never have been so few words used to turn
a whole world upside down. We have already glimpsed

this in the words of Tertius in Romans 16, but here we see the full revolutionary architecture of a new way of seeing persons. Knowing Christ crucified has changed the way Paul sees the "useful" "number threes" of his world. Paul wishes Philemon to completely rearrange his household—and not just Philemon, because this is no private letter. It is addressed not just to Philemon but to "Apphia our sister," presumably a co-leader of the church; "Archippus our fellow soldier," whose name implies that he oversees a regiment of calvary; and the entire church that meets in Philemon's house (verse 2). All of them will welcome back the former runaway with the same personal love and attention as if their brother, apostle, partner, and friend Paul were to walk through the door.

THE COMMUNITY OF THE UNUSEFUL

Every family and every community has the seemingly "unuseful" in their midst. My niece Angela was born with Trisomy 13 and lived with it for almost twelve years. For those of us in her family and household, those years were terribly long and terribly short at the same time. There was no magic that could dispel the genetic confusion encoded into every cell of her body, and caring for her was a daily demanding task, sometimes a literal wrestling match with her uncooperative limbs. There were few simple rewards for all the toil. Angela never was able to hold the gaze of another, never able to recognize her own parents. Her limitations of sight and cognition were too great. But others gazed at her; others recognized her. We knew her, and saw her, and named her.

Angela was one of those whose lives are not charmed—never were and never will be.

It is upon such persons that all our quest for blessing depends.

In an economy that evaluates and compensates us in impersonal terms, the most consequential members, the ones who matter the most for all our flourishing, are the ones whom Mammon does not consider useful. It is the "useless" who matter the most. Because if they are persons—if they are seen, known, welcomed, and given places of honor in our households—then all of us are set free from our usefulness.

If those who cannot earn money, and perhaps are not even able to spend it, are of the greatest value, then we, too, can be free from serving it.

If those whom the world has forgotten and written off are the ones we know and remember, then we can trust that we ourselves will be remembered long after our usefulness is gone.

If we can recognize those who cannot even see us—if we can see them as persons—then we ourselves, so often unsure of whether someone truly sees and knows us, can know that from the beginning to the end of our days, we also will be seen.

If we can build households and societies that love the charmless, the uncharmed and uncharming, then we will be free of our addiction to things that make our world seem charmed, the all-too-easy superpowers that leave us anxious and empty. There are persons for whom magic simply does not work—the uncharmable. For them, the only thing that matters is love. If we can stay with them in their limits, their profound anchoring in this place and time, we have some hope that we will not detach from the real world of heart, soul, mind, and strength, and that we will learn the love for which we were designed.

In our deepest hearts we know that being charmed is unreal. All our lives, what we really have been looking for is blessing. We once lay on a mother's breast, looking for a face. We were not looking for magic because we did not need it. All we needed was a person. One day we will come to the end of our lives. Whatever magic medicine managed to do will have come to an end. Our need at that moment will be just what it was the moment we were born.

And whether we find what we need at those extremities of life—the moments of birth and death, injury and disability, alienation and affliction, violence and oppression—will depend almost entirely on whether we have been part of a community, part of a household, that learned that the apparently least important, the ones who can offer nothing to Mammon, are in fact the ones of paramount value.

For the flourishing of persons, everything depends on the ones who are unuseful.

THE BROKEN CHARM

In 2020, a charm was lifted from the world.

One of the interesting features of charms in fairy tales is that their abrupt expiration is often foretold—and yet the heroes and heroines neglect to be prepared. Cinderella knows that her coach will turn into a pumpkin at midnight, and yet she parties on. So it is mysteriously true both that the arrival of a global pandemic was completely, comprehensively predicted and also that none of us were truly prepared.

Even people hailed for their foresight and futuristic vision were caught unaware. The subtitle of Yuval Harari's bestselling book *Homo Deus,* published in 2015, is *A Brief History of Tomorrow.* In its opening pages Harari wrote, in a matter-of-fact tone, that modern human beings had conquered their three great foes—famine, war, and plague. The next human project, as Harari saw it (following in the footsteps of his unacknowledged ancestors, the alchemists), was a technologically mediated transition to a new kind of superhuman life.

Four years later, it became clear that the hyperconfident opening pages of *Homo Deus* had overlooked a rather consequential turn of events in the "history of tomorrow."

To view the three ancient enemies of humanity as conquered—part of the past but not part of tomorrow— already required in 2015 an ability to bracket out the experiences of the tens of millions of people displaced by war (twelve million in that year in Syria alone) and the hundreds of millions more living at the edge of famine and at the mercy of virulent diseases like Ebola. It required heroic acts of forgetting, ignoring, and wishful thinking all at once.

But these afflictions were so sufficiently contained that when I read Harari's book with a group of students in Vancouver, British Columbia, in the summer of 2019, it took some effort and will to keep in mind the abundant evidence that these scourges of humanity were not quite as quiet as Harari supposed.

One of the effects of the technological charm we have lived under is a loss of memory, an inability to hold in mind even recent events, especially those that spared us and our immediate communities and families. We are the charmed ones, after all, who float through life without the sufferings that other distant, unfortunate people experience. Their uncharmed existence has so little to do with us.

So residents of North America and Europe would visit Southeast Asia in the 2010s and observe the widespread use of face masks in public, but not really pause to absorb the origin of this practice. We had already forgotten, if we ever really knew, that in 2003 Asia had been brought to a halt by the first SARS epidemic. Mask wearing was not in fact an expression of some inscrutable Asian cultural preference but a concrete, practical collective response to a threat that its most immediate targets had by no means forgotten.

Of course, I hardly need to explain this to any reader, anywhere in the world, today. Plague, it turns out, has not been vanquished. It hasn't even been banished to the cruel, uncharmed edges of the world. The natural prowess of the human immune system and our technological ingenuity have blunted the effects of COVID-19, as they have other diseases. But there are many more coronaviruses and other pathogens waiting in the wings.

As I write, we are not experiencing worldwide war or famine. The sad suggestion of history, though, is that this respite is a temporary charm, not a lasting blessing. And there are a billion or more human beings alive for whom even the quietest state of global affairs brings no relief from urgent suffering. They are the ones without access to Mammon's charmed circle, the ones who lie just outside its gates.

There are two ways of viewing those billion persons who do not have the luxury of the magic with which some of us have, imperfectly and temporarily, warded off humanity's ancient scourges. One, implicit in Harari's "history of tomorrow," is to view them as the last casualties of an era we are leaving behind on our way to our posthuman future. We may view them with pity, but also from such a distance that we can dismiss them and believe that their existence has nothing to do with ours.

But another way is to view them, and our response or nonresponse to them, as the true measure of our own humanity. If we direct our technology toward widening the gap ever further from the uncharmed, as Harari prophesies we will, we will actually find ourselves losing our personhood, losing our own humanity without gaining anything close to deity. But if we begin to build our personal economy—the use of our own resources and households—and our shared economy around the uncharmed and unuseful, we will actually recover much that has been lost under the empire of Mammon.

Such a redirection of our attention and efforts would not at all require leaving behind science and technological progress. The created world is good, with resources already discovered—and not yet discovered—to sustain good life. This is certainly true in the arena of medicine, the sector where we may have seen the most unambiguous progress in the last century. The more medicine is practiced with both our heart-soul-mind-strength capabilities and our genuine limitations in mind, the more it can be a fruitful part of the mysterious and beautiful story of blessing that is possible for every person's life, whatever challenges they face.

Medicine, in this sense, was practiced in the premodern period, even though people had no working knowledge of infection or vaccines. The first urban Christians who provided basic nursing care to their neighbors who were struck low by the plagues almost certainly contributed to those neighbors' survival rates, leading over time to the growth of the Christian church. They had no charms to offer, but they did have—and they sacrificially offered—personal community and personal love.

One lesson of the COVID-19 pandemic, however, is

how little medicine itself can do in the absence of such common love. To be sure, safe and effective vaccines were developed astonishingly swiftly by scientists and deployed on an amazingly rapid scale by technologists. The vaccines almost certainly reduced the ultimate toll of this particular pathogen, and perhaps many more in the future. They could easily seem like the ultimate charm, magically stopping a viral foe in its tracks.

But much of what gave COVID-19 its virulent power to disrupt most of the world—especially the "developed," technology-dependent world—was our inability to coordinate action at a much more basic human level.

An ordinary surgical mask is not a charm. It does not confer immunity the way a safe and effective vaccine can. Indeed, it works no magic at all. But it does reduce risk, for the wearer and those around them. And simply reducing risk is a great deal of the game, at least with a moderately infectious virus like SARS-CoV-2. Consistent and widespread mask use, especially early in the outbreak, could have made—and in some parts of the world probably did make—a real difference in the overall course of the disease.

Likewise, the outdoors, open to sky and breezes, turned out to be the very best place to be in the face of an airborne virus. The dangerous places were over-engineered buildings, with their heating and cooling systems designed to deliver artificially controlled environments, many of them with windows permanently closed.

In combining a vast, Mammon-fueled quest for a

technological charm with the neglect of simple, personal-level choices that could have led to health, the response to COVID-19 is a microcosm of our fragile "health-care" system. We vastly overinvest in charms—specifically targeted drugs, extraordinary complex surgical procedures, and measures that we call "heroic" but that actually make sense only if we are dreadfully afraid of death. These charms carry a ruinous price tag. But at the same time, we systematically neglect the basic components of heart-soul-mind-strength and relational health. We have more medicine than ever, but we are by no means well.

COMMUNITIES OF HEALTH

In its proper place—that is, stripped of false promises of magical relief of suffering and enhancement of performance—medicine is a gift. Even though I have lived a relatively charmed life, I might well not have lived to write these words without that gift. A handful of minor surgeries and some carefully chosen medications have warded off illnesses that could have been debilitating or fatal. Those of us who have access to this kind of medicine can only be grateful for what we know about the human body, its vulnerabilities, and the mechanisms that can assist in its healing.

But blessing, in the realm of health, comes from an entirely different source.

Imagine a community that had not eliminated from their midst persons, like those born with trisomies, who will never be useful to Mammon and are evidently vulnerable in ways that the charmed are not. The only way to care for such a person is to grow in your capacity to live wholeheartedly. Meanwhile, many of these persons, including many who live with Trisomy 21, or Down syndrome, offer exceptional levels of honesty and compassion to those around them. A community built around such persons would be emotionally attuned and resonant, capable of the full range of joy and grief.

Imagine a community that incorporated into its very center those at the extremities of life, the very young and the very old. Such persons, who have not yet demonstrated their usefulness or have lived beyond their ability to be productive in Mammon's terms, would remind the whole community that our identity is not bound up in our accomplishments. There is perhaps no more blessed encounter than that between one who is very old and one who came into the world just days or weeks ago. Members of a community that facilitated and witnessed such encounters would live more soulfully, conscious of their own unique dignity and the irreducible love that sustains our personhood.

Imagine a community that included those who through cognitive decline have lost the ability to communicate through normal speech. To understand such a person—to grasp as best we can their needs, hopes, and inner life—requires a vast expansion of our ability to pay attention and interpret another's thoughts. A community built around such persons would live in ways that were—to use a currently popular word—*mindful,* constantly and joyfully extending their capacity to learn, reason, probe, and connect.

And imagine a community that took up the difficult physical task of caring for those whose bodies do not function in typical ways. Even parenting a typical human infant requires physical strength and pulls us through all the axes of bodily movement; caring for those older, taller, and heavier requires real stamina. A community that served such people would live with fullness of strength.

And they would do all this in the context of love. Not love in the sense of infatuation or attraction but in the sense of steadily cultivated regard for the other, putting the other's interests ahead of our own in ways that gradually build up the confidence that we are not alone, that we do not have to fend for ourselves. Not love in the sense of untried and unstable optimism about others' good intentions but the trust that comes on the other side of conflict—not the self-love of young Joseph, the indulgence of Jacob, and the resentment of Joseph's older brothers but the love found in a tearful reunion after betrayal, in which the brothers fell on one another's necks and wept.

The experience of the younger son in Jesus' parable of the two sons—enfolded in his father's embrace, his body pressed against another in welcome and acceptance, his mind reframing the scripts and stories he told himself and had rehearsed a hundred times, his soul being named and recognized while he was still far away, his heart being set free of its burden of shame and regret—would be the underlying reality of such a community.

What would be the health of the members of that community? By some measures the members would be, in fact, *less* healthy than in communities that cull from their midst those who cannot live up to the aspirations of magic. Their health would not be that of those who pursue life extension, those whose pursuit of ability leads them to cut off the insufficiently able before birth, those who use surgery and drugs in old age to conceal features that are no longer youthful and vigorous.

But given that our society already desperately pursues such simulations of health and is still afflicted with population-level endemic disease, such a community might well on balance be far more healthy, even in conventional terms, than its neighbors. Like Daniel and his companions, forgoing the rich food of Babylon but ending up healthier and saner than their counterparts, such a community might in fact glow with something better than youth.

And when a plague came, when the charms failed, this community might be patient enough to take the small steps that it could, not just to protect its own members' lives but to have the margin and resilience to care for others caught up in suffering and sorrow. Such a people might even remember the times of plague, famine, and war that are the inevitable accompaniments of history as times when blessing was somehow present, not because of an absence of suffering but because of an abundance of grace.

They would be the community of the unuseful. And such a community is the only kind worthy of the name.

12.

THE CHAIN OF PERSONS

There is so much we do not know about what happened to the people gathered around Gaius's table after Paul finished dictating his greetings to Tertius.

We can suppose that after the papyrus was carefully folded, it was handed to Phoebe as she prepared for her journey to Rome. Knowing the perils of ancient travel, we can be sure that her journey was anything but uneventful. Did she travel alone, a woman voyager in a relentlessly patriarchal world? Did a member of Gaius's household, one of her "brothers and sisters," accompany her? She leaves behind no further trace in the historical record except the letter itself. By some near miracle, the words that Paul spoke aloud and Tertius wrote down and Phoebe carried survived long enough to be read and copied and read again, making their way from household to household through the network that was forming in frail tendrils along the commercial and colonial paths of the empire.

We know even less about the fates of the others around the table. Except, of course, for Paul. Yet given how central a figure Paul is in the New Testament, it is striking that the biblical texts give us no direct information about the end of his life. Luke's account in Acts strongly suggests that his dream of continuing on to Spain, with the support of his Roman friends, never came true. He did eventually make it to Rome, as a prisoner under house arrest. The biblical account ends there, leaving later tradition to pick up the story. One morning, we can only suppose, he woke up to learn from the soldier stationed outside the door that Caesar's final order had been given. A citizen, Paul would have been given the courtesy of a swift death—tradition says, by beheading.

It is not likely that Caesar himself ever took much notice of the case. Presumably some midlevel bureaucrat would have authorized the execution. If the official gave it more than a few moments' thought, he surely assumed that was the end of Paul and the beginning of the end of his dubious "gospel" and his strange web of friends.

Recognition is a fragile thing. We are bound to one another, to brothers and sisters, to those we know by face and voice, by a loosely woven web, ghostly strands of electrically conductive tissue propelling neurotransmitters across microscopic synapses. It does not take much to disrupt their tenuous connections. Time alone will do the trick, but so will a swift, sharp blow.

In one moment, very possibly without a cry, the man who had once remembered the names of so many friends, the man who had paused mid-dictation to look at Tertius, the man who believed he had heard the voice of Jesus himself in the decisive encounter of his life, was no more. And within a decade or two, it seems that every one of the original apostles, except for John in exile on remote, arid Patmos, met a similarly abrupt, violent end.

And that, one might have thought, was that. For several subsequent decades, Paul's whole movement, his whole parallel household, seems to have hardly registered in the social networks of the Roman elite. We read nothing of them in the personal letters that continued to wing their way back and forth across the Mediterranean, little of note in the official annals of the first century. Those whose job was to know what was going on did not, apparently, consider Paul's movement worth considering.

If they took notice at all, such elites would have seen Paul's fringe movement—*What were they called again? Christianoi?*—as a minor subplot in the drama of the troublesome province of Judea. Everyone knew Judea would soon need to be pacified by any means necessary, as indeed it later was. A series of ruthless campaigns would leave not much more than one stone atop another in the Jews' holy city. A generation later, the fighting would culminate in a pitiless final defeat at the redoubt named Masada. All these events, being military and violent and victorious, registered in the official's mind. Gaius's friends did not.

ALMOST EVERY TIME

We read this history, of course, on the other side of Christendom. We know that the Roman Empire, even as it went from strength to strength in Paul's day, was far more vulnerable than it seemed. The severing of any number of apostolic heads did not, in fact, cut off the new household that was forming even as emperors came, saw, conquered, and then were deposed and replaced in turn. Nor, for that matter, did the ruthless elimination of the Judean zealots spell an end for the Jewish people. In the long run, though it took breathtaking faith to believe this at the time, both the Jewish and Christian movements would have more staying power and cultural influence than anything else in their world.

This is not because underground movements generally are stronger than their entrenched aboveground foes. The crucifixion of Spartacus and six thousand other slaves along the Appian Way brought the slave revolts to a decisive end. Most of the peoples conquered by the Romans, as with so many empires, sank into assimilation without any further trace. There is no reason that Gaius and his friends, and the movement they represented, should have fared any differently. Yet two millennia later, we see that they were in fact part of a long, slow arc of history that continues to shape our world.

The Romans crucified thousands of people, with the intended effect almost every time. Almost—but not every time.

If we set out in our own day to truly restore the conditions of personhood, to dethrone devices and revive instruments, to shun isolation and rebuild households, and above all to recognize the persons who have no usefulness to Mammon and its regime, what should we expect to happen?

We should expect to see no more impact than Gaius and his friends saw. And we should prepare for a similarly hostile reception the more our faith and practice diverge from the empire around us. There was plenty of discontent in the first century with Augustus's brutal form of peace. But the succeeding centuries can fairly be described, as in Michael Kulikowski's history of the era, as "the triumph of empire." The fault lines were there for anyone to see—but so were the iron bars of reinforcing structures of power, more than capable of holding back the discontent of the relatively powerless.

"I am a Christian, and indeed a Roman Catholic," J. R. R. Tolkien wrote to one of his friends, "so that I do not expect 'history' to be anything but a 'long defeat'—though it contains (and in a legend may contain more clearly and movingly) some samples or glimpses of final victory." We are not wrestling with flesh and blood when we name and confront the power of Mammon. Mammon hates the personal, the familial, the communal—above all when these foundational human realities step beyond the boundaries of tribe, kind, and kin and embrace the other as brother and sister. Mammon is happy for you to provide for your family, especially if in doing so you train them up in the way of usefulness, efficiency, and ambition. But Mammon becomes furious when you sacrifice for those who cannot benefit you, include in your home those who do not belong to you, and care for those who will never care for you.

In this way, Mammon's empire will resist the renewal movement described in this book for almost the opposite reason that Rome resisted the first Christians. Christians were perceived to have failed in duty and loyalty—what the Romans called *pietas*—to Rome and its gods. Their "household of God" shattered the bonds of traditional culture and threatened the guardians of the status quo.

Mammon, however, has done a far better job of shattering bonds and dissolving traditional culture than the Christians ever aspired to do. Where we will meet resistance is more likely in the effort to rebuild lasting commitments, anchored in something other than isolated individuals and their preferences. Our households will be accused of violating not *pietas* but *libertas*, the freedom from obligation and dependence that is the highest good of an impersonal world. The conviction that "you are not your own," to borrow the title of Alan Noble's book on this subject, is radical and threatening to the god of this age.

Perhaps the most contested front of this conflict today has to do with the creation of human beings as male and female, essential partners in sexual reproduction, which, so different from the asexual reproduction of bacteria, let alone the industrial production of machines, intertwines our lives so profoundly with others. The vulnerability that comes with the begetting of children, including the inherent unpredictability of conception and human development, is a scandal to a society in pursuit of control. Countless mothers who have chosen to bring children with Trisomy 21 into the world can testify to the amount of formal and informal pressure they experienced to abort their children. Tellingly, this pressure is applied in places with very different political regimes, from China to northern Europe to the United States. What binds these disparate nations together in their disdain for children with Down syndrome is not a single political goal but a spiritual one: their avid pursuit of "what technology wants." Wherever policy is made and preferences are shaped by the dream of escaping the vulnerabilities, givenness, and interdependence of human life, our bodies will be despised and those who treat embodied persons with reverence will be mocked.

THE FRAGILE COMMUNITY

Every bit as much as Gaius, Phoebe, Tertius, and Paul were, we are surrounded by an empire that will do its best to crush the representatives of a genuine alternative community. The end of this empire is not in sight today. It could, of course, come crashing down in the blink of an eye, as indeed it came close to doing in the climax of 2008's financial crisis. But the first bracing lesson of *The Triumph of Empire* is that Rome had its ways of surviving, longer than any zealot would have expected.

So we have to settle in. We have to prepare for "a long obedience in the same direction," to use the strangely apropos phrase of Nietzsche. As the technological world measures effectiveness in shorter and shorter durations and as the unit of time between stimulus and response shrinks in both public life and our own twitchy inner lives, we will be learning to move in the opposite direction.

For a time—and I mean over generations, not years—our households will operate in ways that are more and more strange to our neighbors. We will be cultivating patience, the ability to be present for longer than we thought we could bear. The way of devices is shorter and faster because they ask less and less of us; the way of instruments is longer and slower because they require the fullness of heart, soul, mind, and strength.

We will be cultivating care. We will have those among us who, because they will never become "independent," will require others to provide for them until the end of their days—and those who, because they cannot act or communicate efficiently, will require a depth of attention that cannot be compressed into a text message. We will come to see them, for all the challenges and burdens that they undoubtedly bring into our lives, as the teachers of real personhood and real community.

Our world, like that of the Romans, is starved for love, and a household like Gaius's is the only place you will ever really find it. In spite of generating imperial resistance, persecution, and suppression, households like Gaius's spread throughout the Roman world. They could spread throughout our world too.

With Gaius and his friends, we will come to believe that we have been rescued from the false promises of the empire that surrounds us. Like them, we will be living lives that many of our neighbors long for and that all of them need. We might even come to say that we have been reborn, given another chance at the life we were looking for the moment we opened our eyes.

In one of his more poetic moments, Paul put it this way: Prophecies come to an end; ecstatic tongues cease— even the superpowers of the spiritual life are temporary. But love never fails (see 1 Corinthians 13:8). It is what we heart-soul-mind-strength complexes were designed for.

ONE HUNDRED PERSONS AWAY

The story of every human being's life is the story of a chain of persons.

I am here to write these words, and you are here to

read them, because when we were young, small, and vulnerable—and at countless other critical moments in our lives—someone cared for us with personal attention.

The persons who cared for us, in their turn, had been recognized and cared for by others. Stretching back beyond history and memory, for each one of us, is an unbroken chain of personal recognition and love. Many, many of these chains have been broken in human history by tragedy, terror, and, frankly, evil. But yours and mine, by some unfathomable grace, were not.

How long are these chains? Not very long. Two New Testament writers, Luke and Matthew, take the time to trace the genealogy of their subject. Luke includes seventy-six names as he draws Jesus' line all the way back to Adam (see 3:23–38). Matthew, presumably writing for a Jewish audience, focuses on the linkages between Jesus and Abraham, including forty names (see 1:2–16). While this number is undoubtedly condensed, if twenty years on average separate a parent from a child, it is not condensed by much, since it takes only five generations to span a century.

Two thousand years of history separate Jesus from his distant ancestor Abraham. The rise of Joseph in Egypt, the enslavement of the Hebrews, the Exodus, the conquest of the Promised Land, the judges, the kings, the rise of Assyria and Babylon and the subsequent Exile, the fall of those empires and the rise of Persia and Rome— all this is encompassed in those two thousand years. But only one hundred individuals, more or less, are needed to connect Jesus across all those centuries to the one whose faith was counted by God as righteousness.

I have a very limited knowledge of my own genealogy, so I do not know many of my ancestors' names, but I can imagine a representative of each generation, men and women, standing in a line. Each of them knew the next, intimately, as parent and child, so I imagine them holding hands as parents and children do. I am holding the left hand of my father, Wayne, in my right hand. I let go of his hand, turn to face him, and move one step to his right, where he is holding the hand of my grandfather Homer. I am already face to face with someone who lived through the Great Depression as a young adult. I move four steps more and am face to face with an ancestor whose name I do not know. She lived through the American Civil War. Two steps more and I am face to face with someone who probably never lived in North America but who perhaps heard news of the American Revolution.

Five more steps down the line, and I have already moved a century further back; five steps more, and I am face to face with someone who lived in the days of William Shakespeare. Only eighteen people separate me from his time in this chain of generations. Fourteen people more, and I am standing before someone who lived through the Black Death in Europe—or perhaps whose life was cut short by it.

This is just my lineage as a European American of motley, largely Scots-Irish, heritage. Every reader of this book could trace a similar, and also very different, chain. Only a few links back, at most, are people who suffered terribly in the cataclysms of history, as well as people who acted with great creativity and bravery. Each one knew a world that is now all but forgotten to us.

And all it takes me, or any of us, to go back along the linked hands of those who came before us and get to the first century of the common era—the time of Gaius, Tertius, Phoebe, and Paul—is one hundred persons.

They could fit in a smallish room—one hundred people is, incidentally, the average size of a church in North America. Along the chain of one hundred people, language and culture would change dramatically, so the first would be a stranger to the last in all kinds of ways, as Gaius or Phoebe or Tertius would be to us. Yet between each link in the chain there would be at least enough intimacy to generate and sustain life.

I once heard one of my seminary professors, the liturgist Horace Allen, observe that because most of the New Testament texts claim the authority of eyewitness testimony, all of us who read the Bible are just one generation away from the life, death, and resurrection of Jesus. When we read the Bible, we are hearing of his life and the first-century church from those who were at most one or two steps removed from the ones who could personally describe, with the writer of the first letter of John, "what we have heard, what we have seen with our eyes, what we have looked at and touched with our hands" (1:1). While this is indeed remarkable, to me what is in some ways even more striking is our closeness through actual relationship—that chain of one hundred people.

Someone knew someone who had actually eaten a meal with Jesus. That someone passed on what they had heard and seen and touched to someone else. And only ninety-eight someones later was Sylvia Edwards, the Sunday school teacher who is the first person I remember really impressing upon me the love and truth of God. Only ninety-eight someones later, perhaps through a very different chain, was Regina Wharton, president of the Zion Harmonizers, who invited me to play piano for the junior choir at St. James African Methodist Episcopal Zion Church during my college years, forever changing my life as a musician and my understanding of Christianity's multicultural reality.

And this leads to the most important thing about these fragile chains that connect us to the distant, but actually not so distant, past. Our biological genealogies are complicated things, fraught with as many stories of betrayal and disappointment as of love and care. Jesus' own ancestry included at least one woman who made her living from a sexually exploitative culture (the prostitute Rahab), and victims and perpetrators of rape accompanied by murder (Bathsheba, taken by King David from her husband Uriah). The chain of persons that led to our biological existence is full of such stories. Violation and violence are all too present in the chain of hands.

But there is another story—another chain in our lives—that matters more. Sometimes it converges with the lines of biological conception, but often, perhaps most of the time, it diverges from our tangled and painful family histories. Yet it is just as powerful and, in the long run, makes all the difference.

It is the chain of genuine love.

Someone in your life loved you as the person you are, as the person you are meant to be. They included you in their household—whether through meals around a table, a roof over your head, or the kind of care that we expect parents to give children and siblings to give one another.

They were different from others you knew, perhaps different from your own family. They were less dependent on devices, more willing to be present in the world without convenience. They shunned anything that made easy promises. They had a capacity for patience, for suffering over time, that opened them up not just to pain but to beauty. They did not look for usefulness in others; they may not have seemed to have any usefulness of their own. When you were with them, it did not seem like usefulness was the point.

It is exceedingly unlikely that you are reading this book, and have gotten this far in this book, without at least one such person in your life. I am almost certain you know their name.

And you would not be reading now, all the way to the end of this book, unless you could become such a person for someone else. When you do, you will be joining the thread of history that matters most—the thread of personal recognition, from one generation to the next, which is the only thing that keeps the life that is really life going in human history.

THE THOUSANDTH GENERATION

There are parts of the Bible that, seen from one angle, seem difficult or even shocking to us and yet when seen from another seem utterly empirically accurate. One of these is the way God describes himself in Exodus 20:5–6: "I the LORD your God am a jealous God, punishing children for the iniquity of parents, to the third and the fourth generation of those who reject me, but showing steadfast love to the thousandth generation of those who love me and keep my commandments."

It is easy to be scandalized by this self-portrait of a God who is jealous and who punishes children for sins they themselves didn't commit. Yet there is another angle from which this description of God's character is not only profoundly hopeful and merciful but also deeply in line with what we know is true of human life.

It is undoubtedly true that violence and violation in one generation has tangible consequences in the next. We have evidence that severe stress and loss have epigenetic effects that can be passed on from parents to children, even if the traumatic experiences happened before the children were conceived. Violation, violence, and—worst of all—sheer neglect prevent far too many persons from ever forming a healthy capacity for recognition and connection. The parents' sins, which so often stem from their own parents' sins, do indeed visit their children.

And yet this destructive effect has a fundamental half-life because every generation is born with the capacity for love, eyes wide open, looking for a face. And because no one comes of age without that most basic need for love being at least partly met, the wrongs done to our parents by their parents, no matter how much they may visit us in part, only visit us in part.

If you need convincing of this, you can board a plane and visit the sites of the most notorious traumas of the last century. In the spring of 2015 I spent several days in Phnom Penh, Cambodia. In my own childhood years, a campaign of unbelievable violence was carried out in that country by the Khmer Rouge movement. I visited Tuol Sleng, a former high school where some of the worst atrocities were committed, torture beyond description both physical and psychological. I looked into the eyes of Tuol Sleng's victims, who were cataloged and photographed upon intake with terrifying bureaucratic efficiency. Those who were merely murdered suffered the most gentle fate. The violence of the Khmer Rouge era is inexpressible.

And yet, the streets of Phnom Penh today are full of small-cc motorbikes jostling together as one of Asia's youngest populations, young men and women, buzz through the city on the way to education, jobs, and rendezvous with friends. Their lives are not easy, and their country bears all kinds of scars, including the kind of authoritarian government that often arises in the wake of social chaos. Get to know the stories of any one of them, not to mention the systematic exploitation that occurs just barely out of sight, and you will have no illusions that iniquity has not left its mark in both psychological and sociological forms.

But given the scale of the trauma the country suffered just two generations ago, the hope and energy in the streets are astonishing. The week that I was there, I met with investigators who had just concluded a major countrywide survey of CSEC, the commercial sexual exploitation of children. Just ten years earlier, Cambodia had been a notorious destination for pedophiles from around the world, with almost no effective law enforcement prosecuting or deterring this heinous practice. But the researchers were able to document that by 2015 CSEC had been practically eradicated.

Iniquity does play itself out to the third and fourth generation. This is a biological fact, not to mention a spiritual one. But there is another story playing itself out in our lives: the story, sometimes following our family lines and sometimes diverging entirely from them, of love. And this story does not decay in the same way as the story of violence. It has extraordinary generative power. The most dramatic turning points in this story generate a capacity for love that can last for millennia.

Abraham and Sarah, for all their doubting laughter, answered a call to faith, and their household is still shaping our world two hundred generations later.

The Hebrew people fled Egypt one hurried night and still gather in their homes each year at the time of the vernal equinox, eating unleavened bread and raising glass after glass of wine on a night that is not like any other night.

And on the eve of that feast, Christians believe, one of Abraham's children showed not just what true humanity is like, but true divinity as well. Three days later, having died and having been raised, he met a woman in a garden, looked her in the eyes, and called her by name.

A SMALL LOW TABLE

One winter night my wife and I quietly let ourselves in the back door of a home just a few miles from our own. Our friend Kathy was putting her younger child to sleep; her husband, Caleb, was bringing their older son home from soccer practice. After the children were put to bed, the four adults gathered in the living room around a small low table, set with cheese and bread and a bottle of wine. There were chairs, but we sat on the floor, closer to one another and the food, unintentionally replicating the reclining posture of meals in the ancient world as well as of many cultures today. We shared this small late supper as we caught up on the joys and struggles of our lives, with all the laughter, earnestness, and tears that any honest account of life requires.

We have radically different genealogies, biologically

and culturally speaking—our grandparents were born on four different continents—and vastly different family stories, each with its own beauty and heartbreak. We have all come to faith in the course of our lives but through equally dissimilar paths.

I began thinking about that chain of just one hundred people that connects each of us to the story that is the only reason the four of us were together around this table; the only reason we married our spouses; the only reason, across all differences of history and race and background, that we were having this meal.

I was sharing what I had been reading about mirror neurons—part of the human brain that makes personhood not just possible for us but engrained in us. The chain of persons is not just a metaphor but a biological reality. Each of us has, imprinted deeply upon the structures of our conscious and unconscious selves, the faces, the voices, the stories of those who have been most meaningful to us. We were literally rewiring our neural circuits in the course of this meal, and the many meals and conversations that had led up to it—revising our selves, you might say, in light of the persons to whom we were bound.

And then it occurred to me that the same "firing and wiring" had happened along the whole chain of personal love. I have lost touch with Sylvia Edwards, but she is not lost to me—she is present in a very real way in how I see and love and name myself and others in the world. In that sense, she is present to my children, though they never met, and to the ones I have been able to love. She was present to Caleb and Kathy around their table. And she, in turn, had absorbed and incorporated into her own neural networks those who most deeply shaped her. This shaping goes far back in time—but, when you consider the small number of links in the chain, not so far after all.

How many generations can be shaped by one household who gather around a table, recognize one another, and send one another out into the world?

The householder Gaius and the city treasurer Erastus, the scribe Tertius and the brother Quartus, deacon Phoebe and her brother Paul—they are still here. Yes, they are here in the mystical sense the church has called the communion of saints, but they are also here in the very structure of our bodies, minds, and souls. The blessing has lasted two hundred generations, but it is meant for a thousand. It outlasted their empire, and it will outlast ours. For now, they surround us like a cloud of witnesses, watching eagerly to see how we, in our own time, will restore persons, will name the unnamed, will care for the vulnerable, will play our part in the restoration of all things.

On the day of that restoration, we dare to hope, we will meet them face to face.

But even now, they are here.

And they send their love.

ACKNOWLEDGMENTS

The best parts of this book took shape over three years, under the shelter of three households.

I am grateful to my friends at Laity Lodge for the gift of space, time, and quiet in 2018 and 2019. They carry on the remarkable legacy of Howard E. Butt, Jr., and Barbara Dan Butt, who lived with such extraordinary abundance and dependence, household-builders with countless children. May they rest in peace and rise in glory.

My thanks to the residents of Coram Deo, a home for worship, prayer, and entrepreneurship in Manhattan, for their hospitality during several long weeks of writing in the depths of Covidtide; and to my colleagues at Praxis, who work with me and have supported this work with such patience and good cheer.

I completed the final revisions while spending one weekend after another at the home of my parents, Wayne and Joyce, as they adjusted to new limitations and walked with each other faithfully and joyfully even in a shadowed valley.

To those friends who sustained this work with your prayers, praying when I asked and praying even more when I was too distracted or discouraged to ask, even as you lived through the great challenges and sorrows of our time—thank you: Alice, Jonathan, Karl, Elizabeth, Michael, Caleb, Kathy, Alan, Curt, David, Jay, Tim, Gary, Andrea, and Andy. I express deep thanks to my agent, Kathy Helmers; my editor, Derek Reed; and the whole team at Convergent, who supported and challenged me in the best possible ways.

Thank you to my children—though you are no longer children—Timothy and Amy, and above all to my beloved Catherine.

Soli Deo gloria.

NOTES

CHAPTER 1: WHAT WE THOUGHT WE WANTED

4 **The developmental psychologist Edward Tronick**
E. Tronick et al., "The Infant's Response to Entrapment Between Contradictory Messages in Face-to-Face Interaction," *Journal of the American Academy of Child Psychiatry* 17, no. 1 (Winter 1978): 1–13.

6 **The capacity to recognize a face** Doris Y. Tsao and Margaret S. Livingstone, "Mechanisms of Face Perception," *Annual Review of Neuroscience* 31 (2008): 411–37.

11 **Like Ernest Hemingway's character** Ernest Hemingway, *The Sun Also Rises* (New York: Scribner, 2014 [1926]), 109.

11 **"During my years caring for patients"** Vivek Murthy, "Work and the Loneliness Epidemic," *Harvard Business Review,* September 26, 2017.

11 **Ben Sasse** Ben Sasse, "Our Loneliness Epidemic," in *Them: Why We Hate Each Other—and How to Heal* (New York: St. Martin's, 2018), 19–46.

11 **Prime Minister Theresa May** The Prime Minister's Office, "PM Commits to Government-Wide Drive to Tackle Loneliness" [press release], January 17, 2018.

12 **"Objective social isolation"** Lynda Flowers et al., "Insight on the Issues: Medicare Spends More on Socially Isolated Older Adults," AARP, November 2017. The researchers do distinguish "objective isolation," which creates the greatest financial burden, from the subjective feeling of loneliness.

15 **the word had a legal meaning** George Mousourakis, "The Law of Persons," in *Fundamentals of Roman Private Law* (Berlin: Springer, 2012): 85–118.

15 **Perhaps 20 percent of the population** William V. Harris, "Towards a Study of the Roman Slave Trade," in *Memoirs of the American Academy in Rome* 36 (1980): 117–40.

16 **It was hard work** Compare the description of Saint Augustine's world—a later but still comparable period—in Peter Brown, *Through the Eye of a Needle: Wealth, the Fall of Rome, and the Making of Christianity in the West, 350–550 AD* (Princeton, N.J.: Princeton University Press, 2012), 25ff.

CHAPTER 2: HEART, SOUL, MIND, STRENGTH

21 **Chicago's O'Hare International Airport was called** Benét J. Wilson, "A Fun History of Airport Codes," United Airlines *Hub,* accessed July 14, 2021, https://hub.united.com/united-history-airport-codes-2201918405.html.

22 **"made in the image of God"** Genesis 1:26–28, most famously, but the theme is restated in Genesis 5:1–3 and 9:6 as well.

24 **"We either contemplate or we exploit"** Leanne Payne, *The Broken Image: Restoring Personal Wholeness Through Healing Prayer* (Grand Rapids, Mich: Baker, 1996), 135. She credits Father Alan Jones with the original use of the phrase.

27 **in American English** Standard British English as well—a friend who grew up in the Caribbean notes that his use of

persons was repeatedly corrected to *people* when he moved to the United Kingdom.

28 **there is a difference between "something"** Robert Spaemann, *Persons: The Difference Between "Someone" and "Something,"* trans. Oliver O'Donovan (Oxford: Oxford University Press, 2017).

37 **The psychiatrist Curt Thompson** Curt Thompson, *Anatomy of the Soul: Surprising Connections Between Neuroscience and Spiritual Practices That Can Transform Your Life and Relationships* (Carol Stream, Ill.: Tyndale, 2010) and *The Soul of Shame: Retelling the Stories We Believe About Ourselves* (Downers Grove, Ill.: InterVarsity, 2015). See also his talk "Friday Seminar—Childhood Attachment," accessed July 14, 2021, https://vimeo.com/163619127.

CHAPTER 3: THE SUPERPOWER ZONE

41 **The Japanese theologian Kosuke Koyama** Kosuke Koyama, *Three Mile an Hour God: Biblical Reflections* (Maryknoll, N.Y.: Orbis Books, 1980).

43 **when I was reporting a story** Andy Crouch, "Here's to the Misfits," *Christianity Today,* May 3, 2013.

44 **"Coding gives you superpowers!"** Brian Aspinall, "10 Reasons to Teach Coding," May 26, 2015, http://brianaspinall.com/10-reasons-to-teach-coding-sketchnote-by-sylviaduckworth/.

44 **"4 Wearables That Give You Superpowers"** Mark Wilson, "4 Wearables That Give You Superpowers," *Fast Company,* September 30, 2014.

47 **that the psychologist Mihaly Csikszentmihalyi popularized** Mihaly Csikszentmihalyi, *Flow: The Psychology of Optimal Experience* (New York: HarperCollins, 1990).

51 **swiping over and over on Tinder** Nick Bilton, "Tinder, the Fast-Growing Dating App, Taps an Age-Old Truth," *New York Times,* October 29, 2014.

52 **"drugs of addiction" like "cocaine, amphetamine"** Wolfram Schultz, "Dopamine Reward Prediction Error Coding," *Dialogues in Clinical Neuroscience* 18 (March 2016): 23–32.

56 **"we train on our feet"** Vern Gambetta, "Steve Myrland Interview," Functional Path Training (blog), August 14, 2006, http://functionalpathtraining.blogspot.com/2006/08/steve-myrland-interview.html.

CHAPTER 4: MODERN MAGIC

60 **"Any sufficiently advanced technology"** Arthur C. Clarke, *Profiles of the Future: An Inquiry into the Limits of the Possible* (New York: Harper & Row, 1973).

62 **In Disney's version** "Sorcerer's Apprentice—Fantasia," Disney Video, accessed July 14, 2021, https://video.disney.com/watch/sorcerer-s-apprentice-fantasia-4ea9ebc01a74ea59a5867853.

65 **Paolo Coelho's fable *The Alchemist*** Lisa Capretto, "Paulo Coelho Explains How 'The Alchemist' Went from Flop to Record-Breaking Bestseller," *The Huffington Post,* September 4, 2014.

65 **the lead-off book in the bestselling series** J. K. Rowling, *Harry Potter and the Sorcerer's Stone* (New York: Scholastic Press, 1998).

66 **believed they courted serious spiritual danger** Carl Jung, "Paracelsus as a Spiritual Phenomenon," *The Collected Works of Carl Jung: Alchemical Studies* (Princeton, N.J.: Princeton University Press, 1967), 116–17.

68 ***Die ich rief, die Geister*** Johann Wolfgang von Goethe, "Der Zauberlehrling," 1797.

CHAPTER 5: MONEY AND MAMMON

71 **"help you move . . . a body"** I first heard this line from the late celebrity car mechanic Tom Magliozzi, but it is, unsurprisingly, attributed to all sorts of funny people.

73 **abundance without dependence** I owe this phrase to Jon Tyson, who used it in teaching on Mammon at the 2018 Praxis Summit.

75 **a demonic power** Melissa Petruzzello, s.v. "Mammon," *Encyclopaedia Britannica*, accessed July 14, 2021, www .britannica.com/topic/mammon.

76 **"ordinary embodied human existence"** Craig M. Gay, *Modern Technology and the Human Future: A Christian Appraisal* (Downers Grove, Ill.: IVP Academic, 2018), 95. Gay's entire book is essential reading and foundational for my own argument.

78 **Above the doorway of the Cavendish Laboratory** Roger Wagner and Andrew Briggs, *The Penultimate Curiosity: How Science Swims in the Slipstream of Ultimate Questions* (Oxford: Oxford University Press, 2016), 400–405.

80 **Among the lab's most consequential inventions** Rosalind Picard, "An AI Smartwatch That Prevents Seizures," *TEDx-BeaconStreet*, November 2018.

80 **Epileptic seizures take three thousand lives** "5 Things You Should Know About SUDEP," Centers for Disease Control, 2021.

CHAPTER 6: BORING ROBOTS

82 **Karel Čapek's 1921 play** Karel Čapek, *R.U.R.* (*Rossum's Universal Robots*), tr. Claudia Novack (New York: Penguin Classics, 2004).

82 **coined by his brother Josef** Karel Čapek, "Who Did Actually Invent the Word 'Robot' and What Does It Mean?," accessed July 14, 2021, https://web.archive.org/ web/20120204135259/http://capek.misto.cz/english/ robot.html.

83 **The robot in question . . . GPT-3** "A Robot Wrote This Entire Article. Are You Scared Yet, Human?," *The Guardian*, September 8, 2020.

85 **"few-shot," "one-shot," and even "no-shot" tasks** Tom B. Brown et al., "Language Models Are Few-Shot Learners," Cornell University, May 28, 2020, revised July 22, 2020, arXiv:2005.14165v4.

86 **"ten years away"** See for example Peter Kassan's review of Melanie Mitchell's book *Artificial Intelligence: A Guide for Thinking Humans,* titled "Ten Years Away . . . and Always Will Be," *Skeptic,* https://www.skeptic.com/reading_room/ review-artificial-intelligence-guide-for-thinking-humans-ten -years-away-always-will-be/.

87 **"Nothing in our knowledge of psychology"** Melanie Mitchell, "Why AI Is Harder Than We Think," *Proceedings of the Genetic and Evolutionary Computation Conference,* June 2021.

92 **The 2014 *Fast Company* article** Mark Wilson, "4 Wearables That Give You Superpowers," *Fast Company,* September 30, 2014.

97 **"It is a truth universally acknowledged"** Jane Austen, *Pride and Prejudice* (London: T. Egerton, 1813), 1.

99 **consumes 189,000 kWh of power** Lasse F. Wolff Anthony, Benjamin Kanding, and Raghavendra Selvan, "Carbon-tracker: Tracking and Predicting the Carbon Footprint of Training Deep Learning Models," ICML Workshop on "Challenges in Deploying and Monitoring Machine Learning Systems," 2020, https://arxiv.org/pdf/2007.03051.pdf.

100 **In December 2013, Jeff Bezos revealed** "Amazon," *60 Minutes,* CBS, December 1, 2013.

102 **a journalist named Austin Murphy** Austin Murphy, "I Used to Write for *Sports Illustrated.* Now I Deliver Packages for Amazon," *The Atlantic,* December 25, 2018.

103 **one of these content moderation offices** Casey Newton, "The Trauma Floor," TheVerge.com, February 25, 2019, www.theverge.com/2019/2/25/18229714/cognizant -facebook-content-moderator-interviews-trauma-working -conditions-arizona.

CHAPTER 7: INTERMISSION

107 **Across the Mediterranean Sea in Priene** Craig A. Evans, "Mark's Incipit and the Priene Calendar Inscription: From Jewish Gospel to Greco-Roman Gospel," *Journal of Greco-Roman Christianity and Judaism* 1 (2000): 67–81.

108 **The Roman world ran on slavery** N. T. Wright, *Paul for Everyone: The Prison Letters: Ephesians, Philippians, Colossians, and Philemon* (Louisville, Ky.: Westminster John Knox, 2004), 68–69.

108 **Perhaps one-fifth of the empire's population** William V. Harris, "Towards a Study of the Roman Slave Trade," in *Memoirs of the American Academy in Rome,* vol. 36, *The Seaborne Commerce of Ancient Rome: Studies in Archaeology and History* (Ann Arbor: University of Michigan Press, 1980), 117–40.

108 **the Greek physician Galen** Galen, *De Propriorum Animi Cuiuslibet Affectuum Dignotione et Curatione,* 2nd century AD.

108 **Though the practice was abating** George Mousourakis, "The Law of Persons," in *Fundamentals of Roman Private Law* (Berlin: Springer-Verlag, 2012), 85–118.

109 **the Third Servile War** The standard ancient account is Appian, *The Civil Wars,* Book XIV.

109 **the small-scale violence of daily life** On the close quarters of Roman life, see Alan Kreider, *The Patient Ferment of the Early Church: The Improbable Rise of Christianity in the Roman Empire* (Grand Rapids, Mich.: Baker Academic, 2016), 79–81; and Glenn R. Storey, "The Population of Ancient Rome," *Antiquity* 71 (December 1997): 966–78. On routine violence in Rome, see "Violence, Rebellion and Sexual Exploitation: The Darker Side of Ancient Rome," BBC HistoryExtra, May 23, 2018, www.historyextra.com/period/roman/violence-rebellion-and-sexual-exploitation-the-darker-side-of-ancient-rome.

110 **exposure** Erkki Koskenniemi, *The Exposure of Infants Among*

Jews and Christians in Antiquity, Social World of Biblical
Antiquity 2/4 (Sheffield: Sheffield Phoenix, 2009), 88–110,
cited in Kreider, *Patient Ferment,* 117n125.

111 **borrow the words of the citizens of Priene** Evans, "Mark's
Incipit and the Priene Calendar Inscription," 67–81.

117 **Delivering a letter** Mark Cartwright, "Letters and Post in
the Ancient World," *World History Encyclopedia,* September
10, 2019, www.worldhistory.org/article/1442/letters
--post-in-the-ancient-world.

CHAPTER 8: EXITING THE EMPIRE

126 **Until a generation ago** *Oxford English Dictionary,* s.v.
"impact *(v.),*" accessed June 2021.

127 **120 people** See Acts 1:15.

CHAPTER 9: FROM DEVICES TO INSTRUMENTS

132 **"a bicycle for our minds"** Michael Lawrence Films, "Steve
Jobs, 'Computers Are Like a Bicycle for Our Minds,'"
June 1, 2006, www.youtube.com/watch?v=ob_GX50Za6c.

135 **the word** *devices* Albert Borgmann, *Technology and the
Character of Contemporary Life: A Philosophical Inquiry*
(Chicago: University of Chicago Press, 1984).

137 **Even the da Vinci Surgical System** Cade Metz, "When
the Robot Wields the Scalpel," *New York Times,* May 4,
2021, D4.

141 **Richard Bauckham's fascinating book** Richard Bauckham,
Jesus and the Eyewitnesses: The Gospels as Eyewitness Testimony
(Grand Rapids, Mich: Eerdmans, 2006).

143 **the writer Wendell Berry distinguishes** Wendell Berry, "A
Native Hill," in *The Art of the Commonplace: The Agrarian
Essays of Wendell Berry,* ed. Norman Wirzba (Berkeley, Calif.:
Counterpoint, 2002), 12. I am grateful to Dan Brendsel
for calling this concept to my attention in his talk "The

Path More Traveled: Of Paths, Roads, and the Place of the Church in Christian Engagement of Technology," given at the Center for Pastor Theologians conference on technology on October 14, 2019.

CHAPTER 10: FROM FAMILY TO HOUSEHOLD

155 **it describes only a minority** "America's Family and Living Arrangements: 2020: Table H2. Households, by Type, Age of Members, Region of Residence, and Age of Householder: 2020," United States Census Bureau, 2020, www.census.gov/data/tables/2020/demo/families/cps-2020.html.

157 **Among them are the 120,000 children** U.S. Department of Health and Human Services, "The AFCARS [Adoption and Foster Care Analysis and Reporting System] Report," June 23, 2020.

158 **millions of migrant workers** Miriam Jordan, "Farmworkers Once Unwelcome Are Now Deemed 'Essential,'" *New York Times,* April 4, 2020, A1.

161 **we have too many roads** "What's a STROAD and Why Does It Matter?," Strong Towns, March 2, 2018, www.strongtowns.org/journal/2018/3/1/whats-a-stroad-and-why-does-it-matter.

163 **The sociologist Peter Berger** Peter L. Berger, *The Sacred Canopy: Elements of a Sociological Theory of Religion* (New York: Anchor, 1990).

CHAPTER 11: FROM CHARMED TO BLESSED

179 **Slaves who had run away** Deborah Kamen, "A Corpus of Inscriptions: Representing Slave Marks in Antiquity," in *Memoirs of the American Academy in Rome* 55 (Ann Arbor: University of Michigan Press, 2011): 95–110.

184 **Yuval Harari's bestselling book** Yuval Noah Harari, *Homo Deus: A Brief History of Tomorrow* (New York: HarperCollins, 2015).

185 **twelve million in that year in Syria alone** United Nations
High Commissioner for Refugees, *Global Trends: Forced
Displacement in 2016,* June 19, 2017, 6, www.unhcr
.org/5943e8a34.pdf.

CHAPTER 12: THE CHAIN OF PERSONS

198 **"the triumph of empire"** Michael Kulikowski, *The Triumph
of Empire: The Roman World from Hadrian to Constantine*
(Cambridge, Mass.: Harvard University Press, 2016).

198 **"I am a Christian, and indeed"** Humphrey Carpenter and
Christopher Tolkien, eds., *The Letters of J. R. R. Tolkien*
(New York: HarperCollins, 2012), no. 195.

199 **"you are not your own"** Alan Noble, *You Are Not Your
Own: Belonging to God in an Inhuman World* (Downers
Grove, Ill.: InterVarsity, 2021).

201 **"a long obedience in the same direction"** Friedrich
Nietzsche, *Beyond Good and Evil: Prelude to a Philosophy
of the Future* (Leipzig: C. G. Naumann, 1886), cited
in Eugene H. Peterson, *A Long Obedience in the Same
Direction: Discipleship in an Instant Society* (Downers Grove,
Ill.: InterVarsity, 1980).

208 **severe stress and loss have epigenetic effects** See, for
example, F. Serpeloni et al., "Grandmaternal Stress During
Pregnancy and DNA Methylation of the Third Generation:
An Epigenome-Wide Association Study," *Translational Psychiatry* 7 (August 15, 2017): e1202.

210 **by 2015 CSEC had been practically eradicated** Robin N.
Haarr, "External Evaluation of International Justice Mission's
Program to Combat Sex Trafficking of Children in Cambo-
dia, 2004–2014: Executive Summary," December 2015.

ABOUT THE AUTHOR

Andy Crouch is the author of four previous books; he is also a partner for theology and culture at Praxis, an organization that works as a creative engine for redemptive entrepreneurship. For more than ten years, Crouch was a producer and then executive editor at *Christianity Today*. His work and writing have been featured in *The New York Times*, *The Wall Street Journal*, *Time*, *Best Christian Writing*, and *Best Spiritual Writing*.

ABOUT THE TYPE

This book was set in Galliard, a typeface designed in 1978 by Matthew Carter (b. 1937) for the Mergenthaler Linotype Company. Galliard is based on the sixteenth-century typefaces of Robert Granjon (1513–89).